# The Journey Called Life

# THE Mananam SERIES

(Mananam–Sanskrit for "Reflection upon the Truth")

*The Light of Wisdom*
*Reincarnatiom: The Karmic Cycle*
*Māyā: The Divine Power*
*Embracing Love*
*At Home in the Universe*
*Beyond Ego*
*Happiness Through Integration*
*Living in Simplicity*
*Timeless Values*
*The Path of Love*
*Mind: Our Greatest Gift*
*The Sages Speak About Immortality*
*The Sages Speak About Life & Death*
*Divine Songs: The Gītās of India*
*Religion and Spirituality*
*Time and Beyond*
*Hindu Culture. Part II*
*Hindu Culture. Part I*
*Satsang with Swami Chinmayananda*
*About Sadhana*
*Divine Grace*
*Spirituality in Family Life*
*The Divine Mother*
*Beyond Stress*
*The Power of Faith*
*Joy: Our True Nature*
*Contemplation in a World of Action*
*Love and Forgiveness*
*Saints and Mystics*
*Om: Symbol of Truth*
*The Illusory Ego*
*(continued on inside back page)*

THE *Mananam* SERIES

# The Journey Called Life

CHINMAYA PUBLICATIONS

CHINMAYA MISSION WEST PUBLICATIONS DIVISION

Chinmaya Publications
Chinmaya Mission West Publications Division

P.O. Box 129
Piercy, CA 95587, USA

Distribution Office
560 Bridgetowne Pike
Langhorne, PA 19053
Phone: (215) 396-0390    Fax: (215) 396-9710
Toll Free: 1-888-CMW-READ (1-888-269-7323)
Internet: www.chinmayapublications.org

Central Chinmaya Mission Trust
Sandeepany Sadhanalaya
Saki Vihar Road
Mumbai, India 400 072

Credits:

*Series Editors*: Margaret Leuverink, Rashmi Mehrotra
*Consulting Editor:* Swami Shantananda
*Associate Editor*: Neena Dev
*Editorial Assistants*: Pat Loganathan, Vinni Soni
*Production Manager*: Arun Mehrotra
*Cover Illustration:* Manisha Melwani
*Inside Illustrations*: Yoshiko Sunahara
*Printed by*: Central Plains Book Manufacturing

Library of Congress Catalog Card Number: 2001117410
ISBN 1-880687-46-1

# Contents

*Preface*                                                                    *xi*

PART ONE
## THE JOURNEY

I.   The Four Stages of Life                                                  4
     *by Swami Satprakashananda*
        The Efficacy of *Svadharma*                                          6

II.  To Be in the World but Not of It                                        12
     *by Swami Lokeswarananda*
        Take Life as Fun                                                     12

III. The Concept of Duty in Hinduism                                        15
     *by Swami Yatiswarananda*
        Duties for the Householder                                          17
        Man's Duty to Himself                                               18
        Duty and Attachment                                                 21


PART TWO
## THE EARLY YEARS

IV.  A Living Education                                                      28
     *by Eknath Easwaran*
        Self-Will Versus Love                                               30
        Spiritual Reconstruction                                            33

V.   Spiritual Culture                                                      37
     *by Swami Chinmayananda*
        Immortal Ideals                                                     38
        Relationship to Society                                             40
        Relationship to the Teacher                                         44
        Practicing Charity                                                  47
        Proper Conduct                                                      49

VI.   The Student                                    53
      *by Swami Jyotirmayananda*
            Study                                     53
            Tenacity                                  54
            Understanding                             55
            Devotion                                  57
            Eradication of Defects                    58
            Do It Now                                 60
            Target                                    60

VII   Guidelines for Right Living                     62
      *by Swami Ishwarananda*
            Student Life                              62
            Family Life                               63
            Forest Life and Renunciation             67

PART THREE

FAMILY LIFE

VIII.  Advice to Householders                         74
       *by Swami Chinmayananda*
            Spiritual Education for Children          81

IX.    Parenting                                      85
       *by Swami Tejomayananda*
            The Problem of I-ness                     86
            Everyone Belongs to God                   87
            Our Role                                  88
            Look for the Cause                        90
            Develop the Right Vision                  93

X.     Daily Life as Meditation                       96
       *by Jack Kornfield*
            Moving into the World                     99

XI.    Life in the World                             102
       *by Ramana Maharshi*
       *(Edited by David Godman)*

PART FOUR
# THE GOLDEN YEARS

XII.   Aging and Retirement                          118
       *by Menachem Mendel Schneerson*
          Retirement from What?                      119
          How Attitudes are Formed                   121
          The Steps to Take                          124
          Rejuvenate the Spirit                      125

XIII.  Each is Great in His Own Place                127
       *by Swami Vivekananda*
          Sacrificing for Others                     129

XIV.   *Saṁnyāsa*: Inner and Outer                   131
       *by Swami Tyagananda*
          Renunciation                               134
          Wandering Inward                           140

XV.    The Glory of *Saṁnyāsa*                        144
       *by Swami Tapovanam*
          True Dispassion                            146

       *About the Authors*                           148
       *Sanskrit Pronunciation Guide*                154

# Preface

According to the great spiritual masters the true purpose of life is to realize our divine nature and to express it in our day-to-day life through spiritual living. To help reach this inspiring goal the Vedic masters classified the entire life span of a person into four stages, along with their specific duties and disciplines. They provided guidelines for each stage of life so that we could harmonize our everyday duties with our spiritual goal. The authors in this book clearly show how following these guidelines help to develop our personality and character so that we may gain the strength and courage to meet the many challenges in life. They also describe *how* the outward journey of life affects our inner journey of spiritual evolution.

The book begins with an overview regarding the four stages: *brahmacarya*, (student life); *gṛhastha* (householder's life); *vānaprastha* (retirement); and *saṁnyāsa* (renouncement). The authors in this first section demonstrate the significance of these classifications for our lives today. They emphasize that we do not necessarily have to follow the stages sequentially in order to realize the spiritual goal, for depending on our spiritual growth, it is possible to achieve it from any of these four stages.

The first stage of life, the student life, is comprised of study and the disciplining of body and mind. The authors state that it is only when students are given ethical guidelines through the teacher's teachings and their living examples that they can learn to live in harmony with themselves and the society.

The second classification is that of the householders' life. The authors in this section specifically show the crucial role of the householder in maintaining the society. When approached with the right attitude, marriage is a sacred path prescribed for the sake of the spiritual development of the husband and wife.

The main objective in the next stage, retirement, is to move away mentally from the hustle and bustle of life into a more contemplative way of being. When we perform our spiritual practices with firm determination and mental detachment we can achieve the goal wherever we are. At the last stage, the stage of renunciation, the mind has developed a single-pointed devotion to God, and God alone, and this becomes the culmination of the four stages.

The authors in this book show that the ultimate goal in life is to realize our divine nature, and through inspired living this goal can be reached in any of life's four stages. It is then that our journey of life becomes meaningful and full of harmony and beauty.

*The Editors*

# PART ONE

# *The Journey*

*The spiritual quest is a journey without distance.*
*You travel from where you are right now*
*to where you have always been.*
*From ignorance to recognition.*

*Anthony de Mello*

We have been told so long that in order to attain the non-dual knowledge, one has to renounce the world and the company of men altogether and retire to the forest, and mercilessly uproot and throw away love, devotion, and other soft and tender emotions from the heart. When the spiritual seeker tried to attain knowledge in that way, he regarded the whole universe and each person in it as obstacles to the path of religion, and contracting therefore a hatred for them, he often went astray.

But from Shri Ramkrishna we learn that the Vedanta of the forest can be brought to human habitation and applied in practice to the workaday world. Let man do everything he is doing; there is no harm in that; it is sufficient if he is fully convinced that it is God who has manifest before him as the universe and all the beings in it. If he can look upon everyone as God Himself, how can there be an occasion for him to regard himself as superior to others, or cherish anger and hatred for others or an arrogant attitude to them: yes, or to be even kind to them? Thus serving everyone as God, he will have his heart purified and become convinced in a short time that he himself is also a part of God.

Swami Vivekananda

# I

# The Four Stages of Life

by Swami Satprakashananda

Just as the social life, according to the Hindu view, has four orders[1] so the individual life has four stages. The four successive stages (*āśrama*) of the individual life are the student's life (*brahmacarya*), the householder's life (*gṛhastha*), the retired and contemplative life in the forest (*vānaprastha*), and the monastic life (*saṁnyāsa*). A man's *svadharma* depends as much on his stage of life as on his social order.[2]

The main duties of a student, whatever social order he may belong to, are the formation of character and receiving education, religious as well as secular. The moral fitness of the student was an essential condition even for receiving intellectual knowledge, because, knowledge being power, there is danger in its abuse. Obedience and service to the teacher and contact with his exemplary life were the effective means to develop the student's moral nature. Moral and spiritual life do not grow without inspiration.

For intellectual development instruction may be an adequate means, but not for the moral and the spiritual. It is from living examples, and not from mere words, that one can draw inspiration. From books and talks a student may acquire lofty moral and spiritual ideas, yet they will not be implanted in his mind as ideals until he finds them exemplified in the lives of the great. Direct contact with such lives is most helpful. The greater the reverence for them the greater the inspiration. So says Lord

Tennyson: "Let knowledge grow from more to more. But more of reverence in us dwell."[3]

After finishing his education a person can marry and lead the householder's life if he so desires. The householder is the mainstay of society. He is its full-fledged member, so to speak. The student, the forest-dweller, and the *saṁnyāsī* (monk) are not members of society in the same sense. The *saṁnyāsī* actually does not belong to society. He is beyond all social orders. It is especially as householders that the *brāhamṇa*, the *kṣatriya*, the *vaiśya*, and the *śūdra* have specific social duties. In the other three stages of life [student, forest dweller and monk] their duties are similar.

Hindu scriptures have enjoined two special types of work on all householders. These are the *iṣṭa* and the *pūrta*.[4] The *iṣṭa* consists of five kinds of daily sacrifice or service: (1) service to the seers and the sages (rishis) in the form of scriptural study, (2) service to the deities in the form of offering oblations, (3) service to the forefathers, (4) service to humanity, and (5) service to other living creatures.[5] It is worthy of note that here the individual life is conceived as an integral part of the universal life. Man is considered to be a born debtor. He owes more to the universe than the universe owes to him. Throughout his life he should endeavor to discharge his debts to others instead of clamoring for his rights.[6] The second type of work, the *pūrta*, denotes humanitarian deeds, that is, excavating water-tanks, wells, canals, and so on, establishment of temples, alms-houses, rest-houses, and so forth.

In order to meditate on God and worship Him, free from the trammels of the worldly life, the householder may retire into the forest on the completion of his fiftieth year. He may either leave his wife in the care of his sons or take her with him, as the case may be. As a forest-dweller he should live in one particular place, lead a contemplative life, practice austerities, perform certain rites, and cultivate knowledge. In the course of time when he is convinced that without complete renunciation of all earthly ties and obligations he cannot realize the unity or the identity of the self with the Supreme Being, which is the way to Liberation, then he can be a *saṁnyāsī* (literally, a complete renouncer).

A *saṁnyāsī* is the typical follower of the way of renunciation. He does not identify himself with any particular family, society, race, or country, not even with his body or mind. He disowns everything but the Self. He is always aware of his oneness with the Supreme Spirit. God is his all-in-all. As a man of God he belongs to the whole universe. He is a friend of all. No man or society has special claim upon him. He is supersocial. His entire being aims at the attainment of Supreme Good. The nature of a *saṁnyāsī* is thus described by Lord Krishna:

> Alone, free from attachment, and with his senses under control, he should move in this world. All his diversions, all his delight should be in the Self, with his mind on the Self he should look upon everything with the same eyes. Taking shelter in a secluded and secure place, pure-hearted through devotion to Me, the *saṁnyāsī* should meditate on the One Self being identified with Me. ...
> The sage should not get vexed by people nor vex them himself. He should put up with insult and never insult anybody. For the sake of the body he should oppose none, as the animals do. The One Supreme Self dwells in all individual bodies including his own, as the moon is reflected in so many pots of water; and all bodies are made of the same material.
> Possessed of fortitude, he should not be dejected when he gets no food, nor be delighted when he gets any, for both are under divine control. He should try to secure food, as preservation of life is desirable; through it he can contemplate on Truth, knowing which he becomes free.[7]

The way the *saṁnyāsī* realizes *Brahman* has been graphically presented in the *Muṇḍaka Upaniṣad*:

> Finding the Self, the seers become contented with that knowledge. Their souls attain fulfillment in the Supreme Self. Free from all desires and serene, the wise, ever meditative on the

Self, reach everywhere the all-pervading *Brahman* and at death enter into It, the One that is all. Thoroughly convinced of the truth of Vedantic knowledge, and pure-minded through the practice of *saṁnyāsa*, the seekers, ever exerting themselves, become established in Immortal *Brahman* in their lifetime and at death, which is the final one, attain absolute freedom in It.[8]

Thus, by living the four stages of life successively a man can attain Liberation. This is the regular course. But everyone need not live all the consecutive stages in order to reach the Goal. There may be extraordinary students (*brahmacārī*) who can live the life of a forest-dweller or a *saṁnyāsī* without going through the intermediary stage or stages, just as there may be exceptional householders who can enter into monastic life directly. As a matter of fact, there have been many such instances of extraordinary capacity. The Upanishads lend support to these supernormal cases:

After completing the student's life (*brahmacarya*) a person should be a householder; after living the householder's life he should be a forest-dweller, and after being a forest-dweller he should be a *saṁnyāsī*. Or, it may happen that he can become a *saṁnyāsī* from the student's life or from the householder's life or from the forest-life. ... The very day one has the spirit of renunciation one can be a *saṁnyāsī*.[9]

This view is endorsed by Lord Krishna:

The qualified *brahmacārī*,[10] with his mind devoted to Me, may become a householder, or a forest-dweller, or a *saṁnyāsī*; or, he may proceed from one stage of life to another successively, but never reversely.[11]

In the process of time the old institutions of India have undergone a great change. At the present age the Hindus do not live the four orders of life (*āśrama*) strictly in the same way as in ancient days. The systems of *brahmacarya* (religious studentship) and *vānaprastha* (forest-life) barely exist in old forms. Most of the Hindus today, as it is everywhere, rest satisfied with the householder's life. Yet there are many men and women who repair in advanced age to holy and secluded places to live the life of devotion and meditation; and *saṁnyāsa* is still prevalent.

## *The Efficacy of* Svadharma

An important point to note in this connection is that a man can attain Supreme Good from any of these four stages of life (*āśrama*). Each of them is adequate to lead to the goal, if rightly practiced. In this sense all are equally efficacious. Yet each succeeding stage (*āśrama*) is considered to be higher than the preceding one, because to enter it a greater advancement in life is needed than to enter the other. The fourth *āśarama*, *saṁnyāsa*, is the highest because no other *āśrama* requires such a high degree of spirituality to adopt it; and being the culmination of renunciation, it affords the greatest facilities for the attainment of the Supreme Goal. But the essential thing is the suitability of the *āśrama* to the varying tendencies and capacities of the seekers.

The one condition for Liberation is the complete renunciation of "I-ness" and "my-ness," culminating in whole-souled devotion to God, or in the realization of the identity of the self with the Supreme Being. The various rites and deeds, conventions and insignia of the different orders of life, have value so far as they conduce to spiritual unfoldment. Indeed, it is the one purpose of all of them. Swami Vivekananda rightly observes:

> To give an objective definition of duty is thus entirely impossible. Yet there is duty from the subjective side. Any action that makes us go Godward is a good action, and is our duty; any action that makes us go downward is evil, and is not our duty.[12]

The duties of the four *āśrama* are so ordained that an individual, according to his psychophysical constitution, may find full scope for spiritual development in one or another of them. Some of the duties which are common to all of them are solely intended for the cultivation of the moral and the spiritual nature of the followers. These are enumerated by Lord Krishna as follows:

> Cleanliness, ablution, regular worship in the morning, at noon, and in the evening, straight-forwardness, visiting the holy places, repetition of the sacred word or formula,... looking upon all beings as Myself, and control of mind, speech, and body — these, O Uddhava, are the observances meant for all the *āśrama*.[13]

Therefore, in order to attain Liberation it is not imperative of a *brahmacārī* (a celibate student) to become a householder or a forest-dweller or a *saṁnyāsī*. One may remain a *naiṣṭhika* (lifelong) *brahmacārī* and reach the goal. Similarly, for God-realization it is not obligatory on a householder to leave the world. He has an option in this matter, as Lord Krishna says: "A devotee, worshipping Me through his household duties, may lead a householder's life, may retire into the forest, or (if he has progeny) may embrace *saṁnyāsa*."[14]

That a person can reach the goal from any one of these four stages or *āśrama* has also been affirmed by Manu: "Of all these *āśrama*, one or more, being rightly pursued, according to the directions of the scriptures, lead the true follower, the seeker of *Brahman*, to the Supreme Goal."[15]

To sum up, the various duties of all the different orders of the social and the individual life (*varṇa* and *āśrama*) are efficacious for the attainment of Supreme Good, when performed in the spirit of worshipping the Lord. This has been very clearly stated by Lord Krishna:

> The worship of Me is a duty for all. He who thus worships Me constantly and exclusively, through the performance of his duties, knowing My presence in all beings, soon attains to a

steadfast devotion to Me. O Uddhava, through his undying devotion he comes to Me, the Great Lord of all beings, the beginning and end of all, and so their cause — *Brahman*. Having his mind thus purified by the performance of his duties and being aware of my Divinity he gains knowledge and realization and soon attains to Me. All his duty, consisting of specific practices, of those belonging to different social orders (*varṇa*) and stages of life (*āśrama*), if attended with devotion to Me, become supreme and conducive to liberation.[16]

So we find that *svadharma* constitutes the bridge between God and the world. The fourfold division of the social and the individual life is intended to lead every human being, at whatever level of life, to the Supreme Good along his own line of growth and thus to maintain the entire structure of human society in steady and progressive form.

Footnotes:

[1]  *Manu Smṛti* specified the duties of the four classes as follows: Study and teaching, worship and guiding worship, making and receiving gifts — these are the duties ordained for the *brāhmaṇa*. Protection of people, charity, worship, study, non-addiction to sense-enjoyments — these are the duties ordained for the *kṣatriya*. Preservation of cattle, charity, worship, study, commerce, money-lending, agriculture — these are the duties ordained for the *vaiśya*. Ungrudging service to the other three classes is the main duty prescribed for the *śūdra*.

[2]  A person's duty should always be in accord with his inner tendencies and capacities and his situation in life. This is what *svadharma* means. On this are based the four social orders (*varṇa*), and the four stages of the individual life (*āśrama*).

[3]  Tennyson, *In Memoriam*, prologue p.2.

[4]  See *Manu Smṛti* IV:226.

[5]  See *Manu Smṛti* III:70.

[6]  Cf. St Paul's Epistle to the Romans, 13:7, "Render therefore to all their dues: tribute to whom tribute is *due*: custom to whom custom, fear to whom fear; honor to whom honor."

[7]  *Śrīmad Bhāgavatam* XI:18, 20-21, 31-34.

[8] *Muṇḍaka Upaniṣad* III:2.5, 6.

[9] *Jābāla Upaniṣad* 4.

[10] The text uses the word *dvija*, which means "twice-born." A member of any of the upper three classes of the society is so called after the purificatory rite of *upanayana* (investiture with the sacred cord), when he is initiated into *brahmacarya āśrama* (religious studentship.) This is his second birth.

[11] *Śrīmad Bhāgavatam* XI:17.38.

[12] *Complete Works of Swami Vivekananda* I, p. 62.

[13] *Śrīmad Bhāgavatam* XI:17.34, 35.

[14] *Śrīmad Bhāgavatam* XI:17.55.

[15] *Manu Smṛti* VI:88.

[16] *Śrīmad Bhāgavatam* XI:18. 43-47.

# II

# To Be in the World but Not of It

*by Swami Lokeswarananda*

Hinduism says that the only way to be happy in the world is to be in the world but not of it. Is this not an absurd proposition? How can you be in the world without being of it? There is also the question why it is wrong to be of the world. And what exactly is meant by being "of the world"?

A man of the world is one who is too much attached to the world. He lets himself be so much influenced by it that he hardly has any freedom of mind. If the conditions around him are good, he is happy; if they are not to his liking, he is disturbed in mind. But nothing in this world is permanent; conditions change, change much too often. They may improve, they may get worse as well. A man of the world has all his joys and sorrows determined by the conditions in which he lives. In fact, he is a creature of his circumstances. How can such a man be happy?

### Take Life as Fun

But is there any escape from this situation? Can anyone be completely free from the influence of his circumstances? Hinduism says it is possible to escape the influence of your circumstances if you take life as fun. If you are playing a football match, you can never be sure that you will win. Take life like that. There are so many imponderables in it that you may find that all your calculations have gone wrong, that, in spite of everything, in spite of your best efforts, success has eluded you. This is not to say that you will not try. You will certainly try, try your hardest, yet if you think you will succeed because you have tried your best, you are mistaken.

The question may arise: "Why should one try at all when one is not sure that one will succeed?" Without any incentive, can one put one's heart into the work one is doing? This is why you are asked to take life as fun. Act your part as well as you can, for otherwise the fun cannot go on; everybody must contribute his share and when everybody does what he or she is expected to do, there is good fun, and everybody enjoys it. It is, therefore, important that you should try your best, doing your allotted duties as well as you can, regardless of whether you succeed or not.

But is it not possible to control circumstances to the extent that you can say with certainty that you will succeed? Now that much advanced technology is at the disposal of man, can he not influence circumstances rather than be influenced by them? To this Hinduism will say that your aim should be not only to change the circumstances but also yourself — your hopes and aspirations, attitudes, levels of thinking, and so on. However good the circumstances may be, you never can have or should have all that you want. If you let your mind decide for you what you want and if you are not able to tell your mind to stop at a given point, you will then find that you are asking for things not only impossible, but also things to which you have no right. In other words, you will become an extremely selfish person, bent on having more than what you need and deserve and by means not very honest either. Given such selfishness, you can never be happy.

To be happy one has to be unselfish, be in the world, but not of it. In other words, one has to detach oneself from one's environment and have complete command over oneself irrespective of the environment in which one is.

# III

# The Concept of Duty in Hinduism

*by Swami Yatiswarananda*

The great lesson of the *Bhagavad Gītā* and other scriptures is that the individual as a part of a community is also a part of an indivisible cosmic whole. In ancient Hindu scriptures there is the symbol of a mighty Being from whose mouth issues the Brahmin, the spiritual man with his passions under control, and possessing knowledge, uprightness, and purity; from His arms, the warrior; from His loin, the trader and farmer whose duty is to provide food and means of human living; from His feet, the laborer who performs the hard work of the world.[1] All orders of society are indispensable parts of the whole, like the parts of the human body. After the completion of the stages of the student and the householder, there is time for the life of retirement, and perhaps further for the life of the anchorite meditating in solitude, free from all attachments.

If every individual, in all stages of his life, is integrated with the underlying cosmic rhythm, he will promote not only his own welfare but also that of all around him. That is the highest duty for each one of us. The Cosmic Being is often represented with multiple hands and feet to remind us of the many manifestations of the Absolute unity. Each person is an actor on the world stage and must learn to play his own part as well as he can. None of us have the same part to play.

The American Declaration of Independence states, "All men are created equal." Now we all know that no two persons are alike either in outer or inner life. How then can they be equal? Vedanta replies: the same spirit dwells in all, but as far as mental and physical capacities, and tendencies are concerned, men are not equal and differ greatly from one another. There is sameness and equality at the spiritual plane but infinite variety at all other planes.

The great scholar and philanthropist Ishvar Chandra Vidyasagar once asked Shri Ramakrishna: "Has God endowed some with more power and others with less?" The Master replied:

> As the all-pervading Spirit He exists in all things, even in the ant. But the manifestations of His power are different in different beings, otherwise, how can one person put ten to flight, while another can't face even one? And why do all people respect you? Have you grown a pair of horns? You have more compassion and learning, therefore people honor you and come to pay you their respects.[2]

The Hindu view teaches each man to take things as they are, find out his own capacity, discover the truth of his own being, and then follow his law of growth, his *svadharma*. He will then be clear about his duty to himself and to society. A certain young householder came to Shri Ramakrishna and said that he had decided to renounce the world and become a *samnyāsin*. The Master advised him to return to his family. "Oh, my father-in-law can maintain them," the would-be monk replied. "Have you no sense of honor?" Shri Ramakrishna asked him. After scolding him, he asked the young man to find a job and maintain his family.[3] There is *dharma* for each individual, for every stage of ordinary life, and even the most work-a-day life partakes of the cosmic rhythm. By fulfilling the duties of life in the proper way every man may attain spiritual progress. There is no question of superiority or inferiority of work, or of station in life. Everybody must strive for spiritual perfection. This is the central message of the *Bhagavad Gītā* and is clearly stated in the verse:

> Man attains the highest spiritual perfection by worshipping through his work the Lord from whom all work proceeds and who permeates all beings.[4]

There are two paths before us: first, the path of legitimate worldly achievement and enjoyment. If properly regulated, this culminates naturally in the second path, namely the path of divine realization and freedom from all bondage. One may choose either of these according to one's capacity. The path to avoid at all costs is that of *adharma*, or unrighteousness, which is fraught with passion, falsehood, and greed. If material prosperity results from activity in the world, it should be shared with others and should be utilized for the promotion of the spiritual welfare of oneself as well as that of others.

### Duties for the Householder

In the Hindu scheme of social life the householder is looked upon as the mainstay of society. It is necessary that children should be taught to contribute to the general welfare and security of the society. It is written in the *Manu Smṛti*, "Just as all living beings depend upon air for their existence, so also people belonging to other stages of life depend on the householder for their sustenance."[5]

However, the householder's life is not considered to be one given to sense-pleasures. In Lord Krishna's advice to his disciple Uddhava this point is stressed again and again.

> The householder must always remember that the ideal good lies not in enjoyment but in the attainment of knowledge, as the individual life becomes part of the cosmic whole. A devotee, having worshiped the divine Spirit through the household duties, may retire into the forest to devote himself entirely to spiritual disciplines and purify his heart.[6]

According to the Hindu scriptures the householder has five kinds of duties to discharge. These are: 1) Worship of gods, 2) Study of the scriptures (duty to the ancient sages), 3) Helping fellow beings, 4) Offering oblation to ancestors and 5) Protecting animals. These duties are called the five-fold great sacrifice *panca-mahā-yajña*.[7] And all these duties are to be performed not as drudgery, but in a spirit of service and worship. When one discharges one's duties in this spirit they do not lead to bondage. On the contrary, they help one in spiritual life. Vedanta aims at integrating duty, service, and worship. If an activity cannot be linked with our spiritual life it is not to be called duty. If you find that a particular work is dragging you away from God, do not do it. All kinds of work must take us nearer and nearer to God. As Lord Krishna tells Uddhava in the *Srīmad Bhāgavatam*:

> He who worships Me constantly and steadfastly through the performance of his duty, knowing Me as the supreme Goal, such a one becomes endowed with knowledge and realization and soon attains to My Being. All duties, if accompanied by devotion to Me, lead to liberation. This is the way to blessedness.[8]

*Man's Duty to Himself*

Over and above the five kinds of duties mentioned above, every man has a duty to himself — to his higher Self. Since every soul is part of the Universal Soul, when a man discharges his duty to his higher Self, he fulfils all other obligations. The higher Self of man is waiting for its manifestation, its unfoldment. But it is constantly being eclipsed by his lower self or ego. In the din and bustle of day-to-day life, in the headlong rush towards sense enjoyment, man neglects the still small voice within him, the cry of his soul. As a result, whatever he does becomes in the end a source of dissatisfaction and frustration for him. Even the so-called service of fellow beings leaves him weary and discontented. All our duties must have the unfoldment of the higher Self as their integral aim. Then alone will life appear to be meaningful.

The main problem is that people want to become teachers but without undergoing a strict course of spiritual practices, we cannot become pure instruments in the hands of the Lord. It is He who lives in the temple of the human body. We should first come to know the Lord ourselves and be able to solve our own problems, and then help others. By our very being we can help others silently, by radiating Truth, without their being aware of it. But without having attained any spiritual experience ourselves it is quite absurd to think or talk about helping others spiritually. Once you have developed real purity and non-attachment, you no longer get mixed up with the world, and the world no longer acts on your mind and nerves. And then alone can you talk about helping others, realizing that you are only an instrument in the hands of the Lord.

There is another thing that should be considered as our duty. A little of the student's life has to be continued even after our school days. If there is any break in our studies and serious readings, it is very bad for the development of our mind and thinking faculty. Many people lose their thinking habit when they leave school or grow older. There is nothing as dangerous as loose, hazy thinking. Having lost their thinking habit, they become only men of action and not men of thought. Both should be combined and harmonized. For most people it becomes impossible to take up their studies again after there has been a break, and the very few who succeed in doing so must pass through a period of terrible strain and struggle, because the thinking habit has been lost. Their shallow superficial readings, their light talk, their thoughtless outward activities have spoilt their thinking faculty to a great extent. If you open your eyes, you will see the effects of this in our present-day world: thoughtless, hectic activity without any higher ideal or deeper understanding of truth and the higher laws; activity for the sake of activity which is not much better than idleness for the sake of idleness, however much people may pride themselves on that kind of active life. It is not enough that we go on creating something. What we create must be something good, constructive, not destructive or tending to degrade humanity.

So even if we do not find time to read much, intense thinking must be made a matter of daily practice. So much time is continually being wasted in thinking useless and even harmful thoughts, which may be made use of for thinking along higher constructive lines. There are so many dull moments in the course of the day, and these dull moments can very well be used for higher thinking. Instead of thinking useless thoughts, let us make use of that time for something higher. Instead of sitting in some corner and being dull, we can make use of such moments by thinking of something higher and truer. If we do this we shall find that there is plenty of time for our practices, our studies, our intelligent thinking. Our thoughts should never be allowed to drift aimlessly.

Very often we go and sit in a more or less thoughtless manner for half an hour or so, or read some light stuff or listen to something light and worthless. All this we do more or less like idiots. We even find it pleasant. But the moment we want to use this half an hour for devotional practices or serious studies, something healthy, our entire brain revolts and resists.

One can ponder profitably over the well-known saying of the Buddha, "Come now, brethren. I do remind ye! Subject to decay are all compounded things. Do ye abide in heedfulness." This advice helps us greatly in avoiding useless occupations and random thinking by making us realize the evanescence of the phenomenon. We should make it a point to stress the unchanging Principle in our life and not that, which is continually changing and transforming itself in countless ways. And the highest duty of man is to realize that Principle here, in this very life, and then to help others in realizing it.

If we consciously utilize the time that is being lost in idle talk, in useless occupations and thoughts, we should find more time than we need. Through practice we can develop such intensive thinking that two hours of ordinary thinking may be done in half an hour. There are two things, quantity and quality. If you cannot increase the quantity, then improve the quality — the quality of your meditation, studies, and so on.

It is advisable for everyone not only to find time for his prayers, *japa* and meditation, but also to have some regular studies, some readings of selected passages from the Upanishads, for at least ten minutes after his spiritual practice. Inertia and dullness are two great enemies of spiritual life in all its phases. And there are many people who develop physical and mental inertia, which is very dangerous. When we allow this mood of inertia to possess us, we do not find any time either for our practices or for readings and studies. In such a mood we do not "see" the time, though the time may be there, we become too dull to be aware of it.

Sense control helps us in thinking intensely and in living intensely and purposefully. Why always go and dwell in the sense world? When the senses are controlled, one can easily remain on the thought plane. Why go and get kicks and blows from the outside world? When distractions are removed, we will be able to lead a more intensive and conscious life, and remain as wide-awake as possible under all circumstances. But very often we find that people become more and more dull and inert like rocks and stones, finding less and less time for their studies and spiritual practice, as soon as the goad of outward distractions and worldly pursuits have been removed.

*Duty and Attachment*

We may do our work for the following reasons: 1) out of attachment to people and objects, 2) out of a sense of duty, 3) or out of devotion to the Supreme Spirit dwelling in all beings. It is the first two reasons that often become mixed up. Most people are unable to separate the true sense of duty from attachment. Duty then becomes a justification for our attachments. This is why one thinker has put it, "Duty is the penalty we have to pay for our attachment." At first sight, this may seem a very curious and unsatisfactory definition, but it must be understood from a higher standpoint. The Buddhas, Christs, Ramakrishnas have no duty at all. In their case there is only loving service and no duty. There is no constraint in their activities. Neither is there any wish for gain, nor any for the fruits of their work. The perfect man has no duty and no attachment. There is nothing he has to perform as duty.[9] His is only loving service done in perfect freedom without any sense of constraint or the thought of "I" and "mine."

Duty does not consist in attachment or clinging to this little world of our ego, to our body-mind consciousness. And I am not prepared to call any work done for the satisfaction of some desires — whatever their nature may be — duty or to give it the place of duty. Such work is attachment and clinging to our little personalities, but never the fruit of a higher sense of duty and freedom.

True duty consists in the control of the senses, in selflessness, in loving service, in the purification and the right concentration of the mind, and in giving all our faculties a higher turn making them fit instruments for the Divine. The purer we become, the better can we do our work as a form of loving service to the Divine in all, but we should see that there is no attachment in it.

Attachment should never be given the name of duty, whatever else it may be. Most people perform their so-called duty out of clinging to sensual pleasures in a gross or subtle form, out of attachment to persons or things, but this is not duty. Here we should learn to discriminate very clearly between what is really deep-rooted egotism in some form or other, and what is duty in the true sense of the term. As long as we are not prepared to renounce our inordinate clinging to our little self and its petty desires, our inordinate hankering for all sorts of sense pleasures and possessions, we can never take a higher standpoint. Therefore, we cannot understand the meaning of the definition, "Duty is the penalty we have to pay for our attachment." Really speaking, duty is that which helps our spiritual progress. This should be taken as a general rule for everyone. The discharging of our various duties — fulfilling our bodily needs or helping others, or serving the Lord — should enable us to attain spiritual progress. If we do not make spiritual progress, then there must be something wrong with our attitude towards work or our sense of duty.

There are also people who cultivate an indifferent mood. They are indifferent to everything except perhaps their own personal affairs. But this indifference is often the result of selfishness and laziness. It is a *tāmasika* state and should not be confused with the true detachment of a spiritual person. Such lethargic and dull people are more dead than alive. True detachment, a true witness attitude, makes you alert, and imparts intensity to everything you set your mind on — work or meditation.

Footnotes:

1   *Puruṣa Sūktam, Ṛg-Veda* X:90.12.
2   *The Gospel of Shri Ramakrishna*, trans. Swami Nikhilananda, p. 31
3   *Ibid.*, p. 3.
4   *Bhagavad Gītā*, XVIII:46.
5   *Manu Smṛti*, III:77.
6   See *Śrīmad Bhāgavatam* XI:17.52, 55.
7   *Bṛhadarāṇyaka Upaniṣad*, I:14,16 and *Śatapatha Brāhmaṇa*, I:7.2.6.
8   *Śrīmad Bhagāvatam* XI:18.44,47.
9   *Bhagavad Gītā*, III:17.

PART TWO

# *The Early Years*

*A glorious new era of peace, prosperity, love and amity can be ushered in, if the youth of today are educated in the methods of self-culture.*

Swami Sivananda

Let your conduct be marked by right action, including study and teaching of the scriptures; by truthfulness in word, deed and thought; by self-denial and the practice of austerity; by poise and self-control, by performance of the everyday duties of life with a cheerful heart and an unattached mind. Speak the truth. Do your duty. Do not neglect the study of scriptures. Do not cut the thread of progeny. Swerve not from truth. Deviate not from the path of good. Revere greatness. Let your mother be a god to you; let your father be a god to you; let your teacher be a god to you; let your guest also be a god to you.

Do only such actions as are blameless. Always show reverence to the great. Whatever you give to others, give with love and respect. Gifts must be given in abundance, with joy, humility, and compassion. If at any time there is any doubt with regard to right conduct, follow the practice of great souls who are guileless, of good judgment, and devoted to truth. Thus conduct yourself always. This is the injunction, this is the teaching, and this is the command of the scriptures.

*Taittirīya Upaniṣad* (I:11.1,2,3,4.)
(*From the translation of Swami Prabhavananda*)

# IV

# *A Living Education*

## *by Eknath Easwaran*

In the Upanishads all knowledge is divided into two kinds, *parā* and *aparā*. *Parā* is spiritual wisdom that enables us to govern our passions, to master our senses, and to become aware of the indivisible unity of life that is divine. *Aparā* is intellectual knowledge which is very useful and necessary in dealing with the phenomenal world, but which has very little to do with transforming anger into compassion, ill will into good will, hatred into love. Unfortunately our great universities have been devoting their attention to the development of *aparā* and have been greatly taken aback at the terrible problems of student unrest and violence in the world. Thoughtful educational leaders who are questioning the basic concept of education itself are not wanting.

Vast sums of money are being expended on improving educational facilities all over the country. Certainly education is the best investment we can make for the progress and prosperity of our nation, and any attempt to curtail the educational budget can only lead to the deterioration of the situation. It is good that teachers and university professors are being paid well now. Years ago people tried to discourage me from taking up a teaching career, saying that it is a noble profession but a sorry trade. When I was on the campus, I followed with some interest the experiments being tried in the field of education, such as cluster colleges, student-initiated courses, courses to meet special demands of women, ethnic minorities and so on. All these may bring a little relief for awhile, but they cannot solve the fundamental problem of our educational system, which does not teach students how to live. Thousands of bright young people decide not to go to college because they have come to suspect that there they are not likely to get what they want. In my considered opinion, their number is going to increase year after year until schools, colleges, and universities revise their current concepts of education, and offer students the opportunity to train for living.

*Parā* education aims at the discovery that all life is one and enables us to translate this discovery into our daily life. It leads to the conquest of violence, which is a complete violation of this indivisible unity. Violence has become the greatest problem of our time. It is born in the minds of men, and it is there that we have to establish peace. As I see it, war is organized violence, but statesmen also are beginning to see that war cannot lead to peace and that violence begets more violence.

In spite of this dawning wisdom on the part of some of our statesmen, there is the possibility, when passions are roused and wills are crossed, that war can break out between nations. War leads only to more war. War can never bring about peace. Mahatma Gandhi used to say that wrong means can never bring about a right end. And right means cannot fail to bring about the right end.

Just as violence cannot bring about peace between nations, similarly violence cannot bring about peace between individuals, families, or races. Most of us have a tendency to get hostile against those who are hostile toward us. Thus, when we hate those who hate us and attack those who attack us, the situation can only go from bad to worse. As the Compassionate Buddha said, "Hatred does not cease by hatred at any time, hatred ceases by love. This is an unalterable law."

*Self-Will Versus Love*

Humanity seems to have reached a great crisis that no longer permits us to live in violation of this supreme law. The growth of science and technology makes it impossible for the world to postpone making this ultimate choice between hate and perish, love and live. There is a formidable practical problem here; that is, how can we remain loving toward those who hate us and try to move closer to those who are angry against us? With the best will in the world, we can resolve to be patient, reasonable, and nonviolent, but we know to our cost how difficult it is in our family life and in our personal relations with friends to maintain this deeply spiritual attitude. We know of brilliant men and women, highly cultured and creative, who are unable to have steadfast personal relationships with their parents, partners, or children. It is this precious capacity of being loving and nonviolent that is developed through the practice of meditation, drawing upon which we can learn not to be provoked under attack, but to remain loving and loyal even toward those around us who are agitated. It is this capacity to endure that calms down the other person, clears his eyes, and enables him to see the situation with some detachment. Once there is some measure of detachment, there is no wrong situation that cannot be corrected.

Unfortunately this is not possible where there is intense self-will. One of my most tragic observations on the modern educational system is that, while it develops the intellect, facilitates technology to make life comfortable, and cultivates artistic awareness, it also intensifies self-will by emphasizing personal pleasure, personal profit, personal prestige, and personal power as the goals of human life. In the name of personality development, the ego is inflated to such an extent that it lives as a petty little fragment in a world of millions of petty little fragments. It is this inflated self-will that is more responsible than any other factor for causing friction between parents and children, husbands and wives in our country today. As I see it, education should help us to bring parents and children closer, husbands and wives closer, so that they may become aware of the underlying unity and yet enjoy the apparent diversity in clothes, hairstyles, opinions. For this, intellectual attainments are not of much help.

Walking humbly in the footsteps of the great mystics of all countries, we should try to keep our eyes on the general welfare of all those around us, forgetting as much as we can our own little egos. It is this self-naughting that enables us to make our maximum contribution to life in whatever field of service we may be called upon to serve. In other words, the mark of educated men or women is not how many degrees they have obtained, nor how many papers they have published in learned journals, but how much they have contributed to the welfare of those around them. In the *Bhagavad Gītā* Lord Krishna tells Arjuna that anyone who lives for himself, forgetting his duty to the world, is a thief.

I cannot help questioning the very concept of personality that we have in the modern world. I hear the word "self-expression" on the campus and see students attempting this through many media. With this I have no quarrel at all, but our real personality, which is spiritual, cannot be expressed through art or science, which deals with finite phenomena. The illumined souls down the ages have declared unanimously that I must lose myself in order to find myself. This is why Mahatma Gandhi said that his great ambition was to reduce himself to zero. In other words, when our self-will is extinguished, we find ourselves to be humble instruments of the divine Will. This is perfect self-expression in which our life becomes a precious work of art which inspires and transforms those around us.

All of us have innumerable opportunities every day in our family relationships to reduce our self-will. Instead of getting agitated with our parents or with our children when they expect us to do what they want, it helps to reduce our self-will if we try to fall in with their wishes even though it is far from pleasant to do so. This can be done effectively when we keep the happiness of those around us first in our mind and our own last. However painful it may be in the earlier stages, we shall find to our increasing satisfaction that through this process of self-naughting we are becoming more happy and secure and the other members of the family likewise. Putting the other person first is a spiritual principle that can be gradually extended to our friends and colleagues to the benefit of all.

Thus our real personality can be best expressed in our personal relationships in the family and in the community. The serious lack of personal relationships in our technological society has brought about depersonalization even on our campuses. No amount of elaborate equipment or extensive libraries can take the place of the personal relationship between the teacher and the students. It is the fire of the teacher's enthusiasm that kindles the spirit of the student. Without this precious talent, a teacher is ineffective because he lacks the power to move the hearts of the students.

The true teacher has a power and a responsibility to exercise that power for no other purpose than of enabling the students to live in harmony with society and the environment. In order to reform society we must be an integral part of society. This does not mean that we should accept the drawbacks of our society with helpless resignation. We should try to set right social wrongs in the same spirit in which we try to correct our own failings. The capacity to rebel, too, is a God-given faculty to be used by us to remedy social ills. This is a power which should be used by the students with the utmost discrimination and never violently under any circumstances. Unfortunately for us, power has been looked upon as something to be exercised over others. This urge is a form of violence and results from an inner lack combined with an inflated ego. This inner deprivation cannot be filled by anything other than the discovery that the source of all joy and security lies within us. This is the discovery we make in meditation. It releases vast power for the benefit of society and never for self-aggrandizement.

When Mahatma Gandhi was leading India to freedom without firing a shot — while the whole world was watching the poor little man of Sevagram in astonished admiration — people used to ask from where he drew this immense power that made him invincible. The answer given by the Mahatma was very simple. He had turned his back upon himself, his own profit and pleasure, prestige and power, and had thus become a very humble instrument in the hands of the Lord for bringing about the political emancipation of an ancient country from the greatest power the world has seen. This is real power. In the *Bhagavad Gītā* Lord Krishna declares that He will magnify such a person to make his life a beneficial contribution to the progress of mankind. In short, if our education has not taught us how to eliminate our self-will in the interest of those around us, it has also denied to us the vast source of power that we can all draw upon when we empty ourselves of ourselves and become humble instruments in the hands of the Lord.

*Spiritual Reconstruction*

Our educational system is mostly concerned with the training of the intellect, only a little of the body, and even less of the emotions. It is necessary to train our intellect carefully, but it is equally necessary to train our senses and learn to govern our emotions. As long as we identify ourselves with our body, it is impossible to train our senses. Saint Francis of Assisi used to refer to his body as Brother Ass. He would look after brother Ass, feeding him and washing him, but on no account would he let Brother Ass ride on his back. As long as we are catering to our senses, instead of using them as obedient servants, it is Brother Ass who is riding on our back, giving rise to a host of physical and psychosomatic ailments.

It is good for us to live in an affluent society, but affluence by itself cannot bring us to life. To come to life fully we need an overriding goal high above petty personal motives, in which we can forget ourselves completely. It is this deep, driving desire to forget ourselves that can lead us to complete spiritual fulfillment. … *No educational system can be called adequate to our needs if it does not give us the motivation, as well as the method, to make our life a contribution to the welfare of the Whole.* Even the maintenance of a healthy body and mind is not for my personal satisfaction but for the welfare of the human family.

The practice of meditation enables us to break through our obsessive identification with the body and the mind to discover our real personality. Similarly, the mind too can be trained skillfully through the practice of meditation to transform anger into compassion, ill will into good will, hatred into love. In the early stages meditation slows down the furious race of thoughts and feelings so that we can gain control of them. The experience is almost like watching a movie in slow motion. Over a period of years meditation enables us to sustain our concentration on a great inspirational passage, for example, the Prayer of Saint Francis of Assisi,[1] to the exclusion of every other thought. What is taking place now is that the prayer is being imprinted on our consciousness. The words have come to life, transforming the pattern of our feelings, thoughts, words, and deeds. The Buddha says, "All that we are is the result of what we have thought."

By mastering this greatest of all arts we can enter into the very depths of our consciousness and change our likes and dislikes, our habits and compulsions, our opinions and attitudes. In whatever living pattern we may be caught, however negative our thinking may have become, the practice of meditation can enable us to overcome these handicaps. During the early years of our *sādhanā*, or spiritual disciplines, this education can be quite painful. It is like demolishing an old building that has become unsafe for habitation, but after the drudgery of demolishing begins the joyous task of building a new home on firm foundations. It is to this spiritual reconstruction that Jesus the Christ calls all of us in words that have echoed down the ages, "Be ye therefore perfect, even as your Father which is in heaven."

This is a mighty undertaking that calls for a teacher who has mastered the art of meditation and demonstrated its power in his daily life to the benefit of all those around him. This is the basis of the Hindu ashram, where the students live with the teacher as members of his family. We know from the Upanishads of great spiritual teachers who had families of their own, expanding their family to embrace all the spiritual aspirants too. The teacher does not lose his love for his mother or wife or child, but regards all his students with the same affection.

The much maligned word *guru* in Sanskrit means "one who is very heavy." This is to indicate that he is so well established in himself that he cannot be swept off his feet by a gust of passion, such as anger, on the part of those around him. He is detached from his own ego and can therefore see clearly the special needs of each individual student and can help him personally to fill that need. Often the guidance he gives to one person may be different from that which he gives to another, but the goal is the same. Without this personal relationship, what can universities give which cannot be given by a computer, a library, or a video cassette? The teacher's best medium of instruction is his personal life. Every student responds to this living education.

Footnote:

[1]  The Prayer of Saint Francis of Assisi:

Lord, make me an instrument of Thy peace
Where there is hatred, let me sow love,
Where there is injury, pardon;
Where there is doubt, faith;
Where there is despair, hope;
Where there is darkness, light;
Where there is sadness, joy.
O divine Master, grant that I may not so much seek

to be consoled as to console,
To be understood as to understand,
To be loved as to love,
For it is in giving that we receive,
It is in pardoning that we are pardoned,
It is in dying to self that we are born to eternal life.

# V

# Spiritual Culture

## by Swami Chinmayananda

Civilization flourishes with the promotion of culture, but when the cultural values decline, the civilization of a society breaks down, as we have known from the fall of Egyptian, Greek, and Roman civilizations. The great religious masters of India, using their own ingenious efforts, have time and again revived the philosophical and religious values that India has stood for and thereby arrested the deterioration of the culture. When culture deteriorates, there is an increase in immorality in the country, and its philosophy is misinterpreted, leading to confusion and chaos among its people. This, in short, is more or less the sad condition of the present world. The need of the hour is to arrest this deterioration by reviving the great philosophical and religious values of life.

In no other literature in the world have these values been so beautifully and exhaustively dealt with as in the sacred books of India. In this context we may note the following advice given to the students by the rishi of the *Taittirīya Upaniṣad*:

> The practice of what is right and proper as fixed by the scriptural texts is to be done along with reading the texts for oneself and propagating their truths. Truth meaning, practicing in life of what is understood to be right and proper, this is to be pursued along with regular studies and preaching. Penance, study, and preaching; control of the senses, study, and preaching; tranquillity, study, and preaching; the "maintenance of fire," study, and preaching; offering to fires in fire-sacrifice,

study, and preaching of the Vedas; serving the quests, study, and preaching; the performance of duties towards man, study and preaching; duties towards children, study and preaching of Vedas; procreation, study, and preaching; propagation of the race, study, and preaching — all these are things to be practiced sincerely.

Satyavachas, son of Rathitara, holds that Truth alone is to be strictly practiced. Thapanitya, son of Paurusishti, declares that penance alone is to be practiced. Naka, son of Mudgala, holds the view that the study and preaching of the Vedas only are to be practiced; that verily is penance: aye, that is penance. (I:9)

This portion of the *Upaniṣad* represents the last concluding lecture given by the teacher to the students of Vedanta in their classroom, as they are about to leave the *gurukula*. In the ancient tradition called the *gurukula* system, the students lived together with the teacher during the length of study, becoming part of the teacher's family. This passage from the *Upaniṣad* closely parallels the corresponding function that we have in our colleges today, which goes by the term of "convocation address." The students are given some key ideas on how to live their lives dedicated to their culture, consistent with what was taught to them as the goal and way of life.

*Immortal Ideals*

It must be the duty of the educated to see that they impart to the growing generation not merely some factual knowledge or some wondrous theories, but also some ideals of pure living, and how to live those ideals in practical life. In short, the secret of a sound culture is crystallized in this ancient convocation address. The teacher presents twelve immortal ideals of living and rules of conduct. And in these passages we find that the brilliant students are repeatedly commissioned to continue their study and be preachers throughout their lifetime. The Upanishadic style lies in its brevity. Use of even a syllable more than the minimum required is considered as a great error, yet, here we find in a small section twelve repetitions of the same idea: study (*svādhyāya*) and discoursing upon the Veda with a view to make others understand (*pravacana*).

For this missionary work the rishis never saw any need for organizing a special class of teachers. The preaching activity was built into the duty of every householder. In the pursuit of his vocation, the householder was not asked to spare any special time or to sacrifice his duties either toward himself, his own children, the society, the nation, or the world. But while emphasizing the need for pursuing his duties at all these levels, the rishis asked him to continuously keep in touch with the scriptures and to preach the same truth to others.

The great qualities that the teacher has insisted upon are: (a) the practice of what is right and proper as indicated in the scriptures (*ṛtam*); (b) living the ideals that have been intellectually comprehended during the studies (*satyam*); (c) a spirit of self-sacrifice and self-denial (*tapas*); (d) control of the senses (*dama*); (e) tranquillity of the mind (*śama*): (f) maintenance of a charitable kitchen at home in the service of all deserving hungry fellow beings (*agni*); (g) practice of concentration and ritualism through fire-worship as was in vogue in the society of those days; and (h) doing one's duty toward humanity, one's children and grandchildren, and toward society.

At the end of the section, three great masters are mentioned who had in the past declared certain ideals that were most important. The necessary quality to be cultivated according to each is either *satyam*, *tapas* or study of the *śāstras*, (*svādhyāya*) and their efficient spread in the society (*pravacana*).

In short, the section reads as a manifesto on the ideal way of living, in which every person is charged to live true to his or her own intellectual convictions, in a spirit of self-denial, while attending to the study of the sacred texts and to the spread of culture among the peoples of the world. Not merely by preaching, but also by living the very same virtues and values in his or her own private life. Therefore, continuing the "convocation address," the teacher says:

> Having taught the Vedas, the preceptor enjoins the pupil: "Speak the truth, do your duty, never swerve from the study of the Vedas; do not cut off the line of descendants in your family, after giving the preceptor the *guru dakṣiṇā*. Never deviate from truth, never fail in your duty, never overlook your own welfare, never neglect your prosperity, never neglect the study and the propagation of the Vedas." (I:11)

After the studies are completed and the students are ready to leave to meet their destinies independently as social beings, the teacher gives his exhortation, which comprises, we might say, "Vedanta in practice." The entire wealth of knowledge gained by the rishis from their experiments with the world of objects, the world of thoughts, and the world of ideas has been brought here from the temples and libraries to the homes and the fields. The modern, half-educated youth are tempted to cry down Vedanta as an impractical theory, but this can only be the sad cry of those who have not read this portion — the crystallized essence of Hinduism — with sufficient poise and peaceful reflection.

### Relationship to Society

In this exhortation the first wave of thought comprises the guru's advice to the students about their relationship to society. "Speak the Truth" *satyam vada*. Truthfulness consists mainly in uttering thought as it is actually perceived, without hypocrisy or any motive to injure others. Ordinarily, a liar is one who does not have the moral courage to express what he sincerely feels. This disparity between thought and word creates in his mind a habit to entertain "self-cancellation" of thoughts. This impoverishes the individual's mental strength, will power, and determined dynamism. Such an exhausted personality is too weak thereafter to make any progress in life's pilgrimage.

In fact, truthfulness is not merely giving expression to one's honest feelings truly and effectively, but in its deeper import, it is the attunement of one's thoughts with one's own intellectual convictions. Unless we are ready to discipline and direct our thought-forces to the unquestioning authority of our reason chastened with knowledge, we cannot grow to realize the full unfoldment of our true and divine nature.

Having developed this quality of truthfulness, where should one apply it? As if anticipating such a doubt in the student, the teacher says: *dharmam cara. Dharma* is a Sanskrit word that has no corresponding word in English. Someone translated it as "righteousness", but this does not convey the amount of meaning contained in the word *dharma*. The word *dharma* includes all those fundamental values of life that are universally good in all places and at all times. It is the foundation of all effort at moral rearmament and ethical perfection. It constitutes the cornerstones for all temples, churches, mosques, synagogues, and gurudwaras. And encompasses the eternal duties of every person who wants to live up to the full dignity of the human being and strive consistently to grow into his full stature as a God-man in this very life. In this ampler meaning we may, for our convenience, but not for our full satisfaction, translate *dharma* as "duty."

Hinduism is built upon duties and responsibilities, not on rights. In contrast, the Western way of thought has molded itself upon the principle of rights. Thus, Western culture has grown through arrows and bullets to reach the present, in which nations are threatening one another with atomic weapons and secret instruments of mutual slaughter to demand and maintain the right of each against the others. Rights are to be taken, to be acquired, and to be preserved. A civilization based upon rights must necessarily come to fight. In such a society, the instincts of acquiring, hoarding, and maintaining ultimately upset peace.

On the other hand, a culture built upon duties recognizes the

*41*

right to do one's duty as a fundamental privilege in life. A generation that understands such a culture gets trained to demand of life ample chances to fulfill its duties. Duty, therefore, develops the spirit of giving, not the lust to hoard or the anxiety to maintain.

As the youngsters of the generation were leaving the teacher's presence, they were advised to keep to the glorious principle of fulfilling their duties toward the society, toward their relations, and also toward themselves. The duty-consciousness of the teachers themselves was such that the fee (*guru dakṣiṇā*) was not demanded of the students even when they were leaving the institution after the completion of their education. The *gurukula* system seemed not to justify itself to demand fees simply because the gurus had educated the students. The system was thorough, and the teachers were so confident of the results that they were sure that they would receive the payment right from the first independent income of the graduating student.

As soon as the students reached home, they plunged into work, and the savings that they could manage to put aside went entirely toward the *guru dakṣiṇā*. No one could forget their own days at the *gurukula* and the fact that their stay at the *gurukula* had been subsidized by the former batch of students. Thus the youth of every generation continued to support the *gurukula* system.

After payment of the fees, the students were advised to enter into a householder's life by marrying a suitable person. They were further advised to live together in marriage, enjoying a perfectly controlled indulgence. It was one of the duties of a Hindu householder that he should not misunderstand his early education, with its overemphasis on *brahmacarya*, and should not continue sex-control in his householder's life, because such self-control at that young age could amount to sex-suppression in the majority of cases. He was therefore advised not to break the line of descendants.

The sequence of thoughts as expressed here — "After giving the teacher his fees, do not cut off the thread of progeny" — implies a healthy suggestion as how best to plan one's life. After finishing your education, first of all become economically independent: learn a trade, create a market, and assure a comfortable income. Then, as the next duty in life, marry and maintain the line of descendants in the family.

This is followed by a series of warnings not to swerve from truthfulness, duty, personal welfare, and prosperity. In a world that recognizes no higher values of existence, such qualities may become a liability for the devotee. In our unintelligent insistence to follow these instructions blindly, we are apt to make fools of ourselves. Therefore, the rishis advised the children of that age not to allow themselves to be used by others, permitting others to trade upon their noble virtues. "Never swerve from dexterity," can be used as the watchword for the spirit of living recommended by the rishis.

"Never neglect your welfare" is the next commandment. The rishi advised the students as they left not to neglect their welfare but to acquire wealth; not with the purpose of self-aggrandizement, and not to corner the entire wealth of the society, creating unequal distribution of wealth that leads to consequent poverty and sorrow for the country. They were asked to be prosperous so that they would be able to serve others in selfless charity. The rules of charity soon follow in this very section of the *Upaniṣad* as the fourth wave of thought.

The above ideas of truthfulness, duty, dexterity, and prosperity cannot be healthily developed and efficiently maintained unless we have the necessary spiritual stamina in ourselves and in our society. Therefore, it is reasserted that we must pursue the study of the scriptures and make it our life's mission to spread those truths among ourselves with an irresistible missionary zeal. Continuing the advice, the teacher says:

> Never swerve from your duties toward gods and toward the
> departed "souls" (manes). May the mother be to thee a god.
> May the father be to thee a god. May the preceptor be to thee
> a god. May the guest be to thee a god. (I:11)

We need not necessarily take this idea in its limited sense only. In its ampler implications it can be an appeal of the rishis to the members of the present generation that in their youthful vigor, though they may be inspired to follow progressive plans for a greater future, they need not condemn and reject the past generations of elders in the society. The youth have always the urge to move forward and the energy to drag the present into the future, but in so doing, they should try to respect and revere the wealth of experience that the older generation has accumulated as a result of their own long-lived lives.

The last generation lingering among us need not be conceived as the sole authority, but at the same time, they need not be totally rejected and discarded. The rishi means that the youth should respect their elders, but at the same time they should not lead their lives in slavish obedience to them. Therefore:

> Let only those actions that are free from blemishes be per-
> formed — and not others. You must follow only those virtu-
> ous actions, which are irreproachable — and not others.
> (I:11)

### Relationship to the Teacher

At the conclusion of this thought-wave, the declaration of the teacher gains a sincerity that is almost unequalled in any other religious literature in the world, both in its modesty and in its selfless dedication to Truth. Philosophy is a subjective science, and its blessing can be gained only by actually living it. Apart from its logic and reason, the theory must have the dynamism of the teacher behind it to inspire the students at all times. Reverence and respect for the teacher has to be there because the moment suspicion and doubt creeps into our minds regarding the purity and sincerity of the teacher, the philosophy that is taught becomes immediately impotent in our hearts. Therefore the teacher says, "Follow only the irreproachable qualities in us."

This does not mean that the teacher is full of vices, but the rishi is extra careful to avoid all possibilities of any misjudgement. Even when an individual has no weakness, it is possible that an observer may project his own mental evaluations on him and come to criticize and condemn the other. As a remedy to all such mental drawbacks, the teacher, accepting this natural weakness in man, exhorts the student to follow only the purest qualities and habits of the teacher. If there be an unhealthy trait that the teacher exhibits, it should not be copied or followed by the student.

This portion clearly shows the attitude that the teachers maintained in the presence of their students. They did not for a moment pose as superhuman beings, or as paragons of purity, strength, or divinity. They behaved among the students as though they were mortals with all possible weaknesses that a mortal is heir to.

Wearing this look of the ordinary and behaving as any ordinary mortal, these men of perfection faced their students. This, in fact, was the secret of their success in spreading the transcendental wisdom among people living amid life's contentions in their day-to-day existence.

The greater the teacher and the firmer his realization, the easier he comes down to move shoulder to shoulder with the students in a spirit of comradeship and friendship. The formalities of distance between the teacher and the taught are insisted upon and maintained only by those uncertain masters who do not have the confidence in their own knowledge or the clarity to remember their own days of confusion.

Continuing the "convocation address," in the fourth wave of thought, the teacher's declaration codifies the relationship of his students with the other gurus in the land, who are equally great, if not greater, than their own teachers. There was no spirit of rivalry among the teachers; in fact, they all worked as a team, serving as preachers and nourishing the culture. But it is only natural that students in their over-enthusiasm and devotion to their guru, come to look down with contempt upon other teachers. This sectarian attitude and preferential reverence are looked down upon with a reproachful eye by the rishis of old. They advised their students to follow a healthier and more tolerant attitude. Therefore:

> You must not even breathe a word when those who are more distinguished than you are in discussion on spiritual matters (or, you must offer a seat to superiors and worship them with acts and reverence and love). (I:11)

The arrangement of Sanskrit words of this verse here — *tvayā' sanena praśvasitavyam* — is a masterly manipulation of sounds in such a way that in themselves they can be made to mean two ideas, both of which are instructions to the student. *Tvayā +āsanena + praśvasitavyam* is one way of dissolving the words, in which case they mean, "The master should be entertained with a seat and other things provided by you." The same can be dissolved as *tvayā + asane + na + praśvasitavyam*, in which case they mean, "Not even a word should be breathed out by you when they are seated in their assembly for discussion."

In the former case, it is advice on how you should receive and entertain all teachers with respect and devotion. And in the latter case, it is a prescription of the code of behavior that one should observe in an assembly of teachers who are discussing philosophical matters among themselves. The idea is that you must be all ears and eyes when the wise talk, and not be full of noise and tongue. When such teachers discuss, there are plenty of ideas that can be absorbed, discussed, and properly assimilated later on. If one were to start discussion and arguments in the very beginning, one is apt to lose oneself in a morass of words.

*Practicing Charity*

Continuing the address to the students, the rishi adds:

> Gifts should be given with faith; they should never be given
> without faith; they should be given in plenty, with modesty
> and with sympathy. (I:11)

As we have noticed earlier, the Hindu culture is essentially
based upon the sacrifice implied in duty and not upon acquisi-
tion implied in a way of life based on rights. Hinduism recognizes the householder's existence only as a necessary training in
curbing his animalism and purifying him for the greater heights
of spirituality. Cultural perfection is the goal. Every breath in the
individual, every activity in his life, and every thought in him is
marshaled and disciplined to bring out the symphony of the perfect spiritual culture. As such, the householder was trained to
live a life of earning and spending, mating and breeding, building and keeping, only as a field of activity for him to train himself in the values of love, kindness, service, and charity. Ultimately the individual was valued upon the spirit of sacrifice he
could show toward the finite, when the call of the Infinite
reached him.

Naturally, therefore, the teacher has to give some instruction
as to how charity can best be practiced. In the name of charity
many a thing is ordinarily done in society, which destroys both
the giver and recipient. The giver gains in vanity, while the recipient becomes an irredeemable idler and a moral wreck. In
order to avoid such social suicide, the master had to instruct the
students on the "laws of giving," lest charity should kill the soul
of this consummate social law.

*Gifts should be given with faith:* Faith is not what we generally understand it to mean. In society faith is generally understood as some idea to be swallowed without questioning, without inquiry. To be under the intellectual tyranny of an individual
or a class is not faith according to Vedanta. This has been made

clear in *Vivekacūḍāmaṇi* by Shri Shankara. Shankara says that to judge and understand the full significance of the advice of teachers and the depth of the declarations in the sacred textbooks, and thereafter to struggle constantly in our thoughts and activities to attune ourselves to these intellectual judgments, is called faith.

Therefore, charity is acceptable only when it is in line with our own independent intellectual beliefs and convictions. Unless we are convinced of the nobility of the cause and unless we have come to a correct and independent judgment upon its worthiness, charity should not be practiced. There is a school of intellectual idlers who believe that our charity must be as open and as free as the fruit trees in an orchard that give their fruits to all without questioning. Such indiscriminate charity is not acceptable to the science of Vedanta, which is not trying to cultivate fruit trees. Its aim is to cultivate the thinking animal called "man." Therefore, the rishi pointedly condemns the opposite idea by the positive declaration, "Gifts should not be given without faith." Every benefactor has the right, even the duty, to inquire into the righteousness of the cause he is trying to patronize.

Again, a miserly giving will not benefit either the giver or the receiver, and therefore it is said that having come to judge a cause to be deserving, give it your entire patronage: "Give in plenty, give with both hands."

However, charity can bring feelings of egoism and vanity. These are avoided by instructions to give with modesty. There are yet others who may have the intellectual vision to judge the cause they are patronizing, the large-heartedness to give in plenty, with all modesty that has been required of them, and yet, they may not have the necessary element of love to feel a deep sympathy with the cause that they happen to patronize. The rishi is here advising that we should not on any score ignore this most essential factor in charity. To give without sympathy is as futile as to paint a picture with black ink on a blackboard!

Sympathy generates love, compelling us to seek an identity with the cause, without it we will not be spiritually evolving along the path of charity. Unless charity is honeyed with the spirit of love and the joy of identification it will only constrict the heart and obstruct our growth.

Hence we are warned against all charity without sympathy with the cause. To throw the smallest coin to a helpless beggar and to make him struggle hard in picking it up from the wayside dirt with his half-eaten leprous fingers is no charity at all.

*Proper Conduct*

Coming to the end of the "convocation address" given to the students, the rishi says:

> Now if there should arise any doubt regarding your actions or any uncertainty in respect of your conduct in life, you should act in those matters exactly as those *brāhmaṇas* there who are thoughtful, religious, not set on by others, not cruel, and are devoted to *dharma*.
>
> And now with regard to those who are falsely accused of some crime, you should conduct yourselves exactly in the same manner as do the *brāhmaṇas* there, who are thoughtful, religious, not set on by others, not cruel, and are devoted to *dharma*. (I:11)

In the thick of life's battle, situations may arise in which there may be a doubt in your mind as to what is the ideal way to live. In all such cases the youngster is advised to follow other elderly members of the society who are the accredited champions of the culture.

The cultural perfection should not be the only qualification necessary to make a man perfect enough to be followed by others. He must be thoughtful: That means that he must be one who is not blindly following the *śāstras*, but is capable of independent thinking and correct judgment. He must not be one who is merely secular in his concept, but one who has respect and reverence for the sanctity of the sacred. A true Brahmin is one who is not only a man of independent judgment and is truly religious, but also one who has the full freedom to express his ideas.

An ideal Brahmin does not court anyone and is not cruel. He must be a self-dedicated champion of the greater values of life as explained in the immortal scriptures. Such men of dedicated life, firmly established in their ideas and stoutly independent, are the true sons of the Hindu culture, and the student is asked to follow them whenever there is a doubt regarding either action or conduct.

Regarding rituals, there are some fundamental doubts regarding the various rules. In all such cases the student has been asked to follow what the ideal local Brahmin follows.

There may be doubts regarding man's conduct, for instance, in a country like India, which incorporates in its vast embrace a variety of geographical conditions, habits and customs, flora and fauna, we find that even contrary and opposite conduct is recognized as ethical and moral in different parts of the country. In these circumstances it is possible that the student has doubts regarding the right conduct, but in all such matters the student is directed to follow the eminent men of culture in the community.

> This is the command. This is the teaching. This is the secret of the Vedas. This is the commandment. This should be observed. Verily, having understood this fully, one must act in the way taught above, continuously, until the last — and not otherwise. (I:11)

With this wave of thought, the master concludes his discourse. When we follow merely the word-meaning, we are apt to misjudge these words as a vain repetition of similar words already used, conveying almost the same sense. But on closer analysis we can discover that in the dramatic layout of the Upanishads, as a conversation between the teacher and the taught, these words declare the character of the student as well as the temperament of the teacher.

In conclusion the teacher declares, "This is the command" (*ādeśa*). In the next sentence he amends it by a much milder term, "This is the advice" (*upadeśa*). Within this context, it should be amply clear to any reader what exactly must have made the teacher amend his words. As soon as he declared that this is the "command," in spite of their reverence to the guru, the students — temperamentally not very willing to accept a command on ethical and moral rules from anyone, even if it be from their own guru, unless he pauses to explain and make them understand the logic of it — seemed to have expressed a revolting look. The attitude of their intellectual dissatisfaction might have expressed itself in the sparkling eyes of the young students, and so the guru dilutes his emphasis by his amendment.

Again, the discriminative intellects of the Vedic generation even in their youthful days were audacious enough to question the teachers until they got complete satisfaction, and the teachers also never misunderstood their students' behavior. They, on the other hand, always expected and encouraged all intellectual honesty and freedom in their students. Seeing this healthy sign of revolt against an individual's intellectual dictatorship, especially in moral and ethical values, the teacher again appealed to them to accept what he said, since his arguments were in no sense a mere intellectual hypothesis of his own independent intellectual calculations, but were the declarations of the Veda (*Upaniṣad*).

Those who understand and enter into the spirit of the Vedas, understand that the declarations of the Vedas are no subject matter for doubt, since they are all declarations of the saints and sages who report their own transcendental experiences, rather than enunciate pronouncements with their finite and limited intellects.

Once the teacher remembered that what he had declared was the *cream* of Hinduism, as declared by the endless hierarchy of divine masters, he gained a self-confidence, as it were, in himself and exploded to say that this is the commandment of the Lord, the very Creator of life.

The above passages, starting with *satyam vada*, consisting of twenty-five items and divisible into six waves of thought, constitute the sacred commandments of Hinduism. The waves of thought as indicated in this section are advice regarding (1) the individual himself, (2) his relationship with others, (3) his right action in the world, (4) his attitude toward the eminent men of culture, (5) the laws of charity, and (6) his duty to follow the eminent living men of his own times.

In the seventh wave of thought, the teacher concludes by saying that these commandments are to be followed diligently by every intelligent seeker who lives for a higher cultural purpose. In short, over the shoulders of the students, as it were, the rishi is addressing the entire community to follow these commandments and bring about the perfect cultural and spiritual unfoldment in themselves and in the society.

# VI

# *The Student*

## *by Swami Jyotirmayananda*

Since being a student is very demanding and time consuming, I have devised a simple method for remembering certain points that will help you to succeed in your studies as well as in life. All you have to do is simply think of the letters of the word "student": S-T-U-D-E-N-T.

*Study*

Study has two aspects: academic study and the perpetual study of life. You are a student as long as you live, until you breathe your last breath. At every moment you are learning something that you did not know before. The eagerness to be open to learning must never stop. As Shakespeare wrote, "There are sermons in stones, and lessons in running brooks." And as the *Bhagavad Gītā* teaches, "Every leaf of the cosmic tree is a Veda — a source of knowledge."

In your academic studies, you must study systematically, regularly, and with self-effort. As a student, you cannot depend on anyone else. It is you who must study and learn; it is you who must prepare for examinations. It would be quite absurd to call a friend and ask him to do your assignments, saying, "Please study this history lesson for me. I'm too busy to do it!"

As a source of inspiration, reflect on the following story about the early years of an ancient saint: There was once a boy who, prior to becoming a saint, was a very poor student. Because he had to work all day, the only time he was able to study was at night. Well one night he could not find sufficient oil to burn his lamp, so he went to bed in a state of frustration. When he finally fell asleep, an angel appeared in his dream and said, "I will give you all the knowledge in the world. All you have to do is open your mouth and I will spit the knowledge into it." The boy became upset and said, "No, please, that is not how I want to attain knowledge. I just want oil for my lamp so that I can study by myself and acquire knowledge with dignity."

Actually, the angel was just testing the poor student and because he was so pleased by the boy's response, he blessed him. Consequently, the boy became a great personality.

This story emphasizes the importance of depending only on yourself. With such a spirit of self-dependence, you too can become an excellent student as well as a great spiritual personality.

Believing in the power of your own self-effort, try to be organized in your studying. Before going to class, always try to prepare ahead for the next lecture. Glance through that subject and have an outline of the information. When you are prepared, your mind has a special capacity to attend to everything you hear. Otherwise, when you listen to a lecture for which you are not prepared, your mind goes blank. Consequently, you become upset and console yourself with the thought, "It is all right, even though I don't have the faintest idea what is going on right now, I'll figure it all out when I get home."

Being a successful student is a great art, one that does not require you to have your head in books day and night. If you manage your time well, you can be prepared in an organized way. Therefore, it is not the quantity of time that you study, but the quality. So study well!

*Tenacity*

Even though you may be weak in a certain subject, do not feel defeated — try again and again. If your effort is sustained with faith, you will succeed with the proper help and guidance. With tenacity, you can do amazing things. Nothing is impossible for anyone. So never for a moment accept the erroneous notion, "I am not meant for this!"

Suppose, for example, that you had to address your class-mates by giving a short talk. You prepare your speech, but the moment you get to the podium you begin to tremble and your voice starts to waver. When you have finally gotten through it, someone tells you that you are not meant to speak publicly — "you don't have what it takes." This is totally wrong. In the initial stage of all study, there is always a little wavering in your heart, a little diffidence. Yet everyone has the capacity to over-come this initial weakness. If you continue with tenacity, you will realize that every subject becomes interesting and engross-ing — a form of exploration.

The idea that a project must go smoothly from beginning to end is wrong. No one becomes a hero in a battle unless he en-counters some difficulty, some smack on the head! Therefore, tenacity must be adopted with great tenaciousness!

*Understanding*

The great secret of happiness lies in understanding, and under-standing means many things. You must have a relaxed mind so that you can understand the academic subjects you are studying in school. You must understand yourself, other people, and you must understand the meaning of the events in your life. As you become wiser and more patient, you must learn to avoid the misunderstandings that waste so much human time and energy.

As a simple illustration of such misunderstanding, reflect upon this story about a farmer and his ax: There was once a farmer who was cutting wood with an ax. He had to go into his house for just a moment so he left his ax outside. When he came out again, he could not find the ax.

The farmer looked around and saw that a young man was

walking near the house that was right across the way from his. He then thought to himself, "It must be him; he must have stolen my ax." The more the farmer looked at him, the more convinced he became that the young man was guilty. The farmer thought to himself, "Why, he not only looks like a thief, he even walks like a thief!" The more the farmer thought about it, the more agitated he became.

While he was getting all worked up, he suddenly turned around and, lo and behold, he saw the ax. In his rush to go into the house, he had apparently let it slip behind the door.

Once again he looked at the young man across the way. Only this time he thought to himself, "Surely he's a good person, for he not only looks like a good person, he even walks like a good person."

This humorous story reflects how quickly attitudes can change. When you misunderstand a situation, you interpret it in a faulty way. However, when you gain a correct understanding, you then interpret the situation in an entirely different way.

Understanding yourself and other human beings is a great art. It is much easier to be a student of botany or astronomy or grammar than to be a student of human nature. A human being is the most mysterious and profound being. Understanding human beings and relating to others in a harmonious way are challenges that continue day by day.

Understanding the meaning of life's events and developing a correct attitude toward adversity and prosperity are also vitally important challenges for every student of life. "Why," the mind asks, "should life present difficult situations before me?" Not finding the answer, it sinks in despair and depression and frustration.

However, if you tried to imagine what would happen to you if there were no difficult situations, if there were only prosperity, if everything happened according to your liking — you would realize that such a life would leave you like a spineless jellyfish!

To understand this better, look at a rosebush. Just as the

thorns are absolutely necessary for the existence of this wonderful flower so, too, adversity is absolutely needed in your life. Just as each thorn allows the sap of the plant to be contained and evaporation to be controlled so, too, each adversity allows the "sap" of your inner strength to be revealed and contained. As that "sap" accumulates, it eventually unfolds all the beautiful roses — the sublime Divine qualities — of your personality.

Remembering the importance of having proper understanding will lead you to a philosophical insight into yoga as well. The entire study of yoga philosophy is a matter of promoting understanding: understanding yourself, understanding the world, understanding your relationship to everyone and everything around you.

### Devotion

In the Upanishads there is a message given to students which states, "Let your mother be your God" *Mātṛ devo bhava*; "Let your father be your God" *Pitṛ devo bhava*; "Let your teacher be your God" *Ācārya devo bhava*. If we take this teaching one step further, we would assert, "Let God be your God" *Deva devo bhava*.

Although relating to God is your ultimate goal, you move towards Him in stages by developing Divine love towards those closest to you in family and society. Your parents are first. Apart from loving them in the basic human way, you develop the spiritual feeling that God is working through them.

In the Vedic culture, when a child first wakes up in the morning, he goes to his parents. He touches the feet of his mother and she blesses him; he touches the feet of his father and he blesses him. What is recognized in this act is that God is working through every individual. The child who is worshiping recognizes God in his mother and father. In turn, the parents recognize that it is God within them who is blessing the child who is showing humility and reverence.

Developing the art of devotion begins at home. You love God by serving your elders, such as your mother, your father, your grandparents, and so on. When you get older, you love God by serving your teachers.

Whenever you learn from a teacher, regardless of the subject, you should develop a special attitude of reverence and humility, so that his or her heart is in communion with yours. This deeper relation between teacher and student is the basis of receiving the highest form of education and culture. But from a more advanced point of view, "teacher" refers to a spiritual preceptor, or *guru* — one who guides you on that special path leading to Liberation.

Devotion must be nurtured little by little in your daily life through prayer, repetition of *mantra* (a sacred Divine name or a mystic formula such as Om, Rama, Krishna, or any sacred name according to your faith), and meditation upon the form of your deity. There are different forms of worship in every religion, but love of God is the same. That love of God has to be developed by a student, for it is the basis for prosperity and higher attainment.

You may accumulate great wealth, fame, and power during your life, but if you do not have love of God flowing through your heart, life is meaningless. Some day you will age and you will no longer be able to enjoy the things you possess. Without devotion to God, you will face absolute despair and loneliness. But if you feel the Divine Presence within you, even when you age, even when death knocks at your door, your mind will be filled with peace and joy. Thus, devotion is the great treasure that makes all else meaningful.

*Eradication of Defects*

Eradication of vices and cultivation of virtues will become possible if you develop the art of introspection. Do not waste your time looking for defects in others. Rather, look within yourself. Every evening, introspect by asking yourself if and how you went wrong: "Did I complete my assignments? Did I react unnecessarily in a certain situation? Did I say something to a friend or classmate that I shouldn't have?" It might even be a good idea to keep a diary and note what you did wrong; then, resolve to remedy the situation.

Never fill your mind with regret and sorrow over the defects you discover in your personality. Errors are natural in human development. A child must fall many times in order to learn how to walk upright. However, do not condone your errors either. Rather, face your errors with boldness! Eradicating vices and developing virtuous qualities must be constant and heroic projects throughout your life.

By introspecting, you will discover certain defects in your personality (like irritability, jealousy, anger, and so on) that tend to persist. There is an art to overcoming these defects; it does not require any form of deep psychoanalysis. Whether or not it is a result of the slap your mother gave you when you were four years old for breaking her favorite vase is not important. When and how you developed negative personality traits do not matter. What is important is that you learn the art of eradicating them.

You must gradually understand that deep down your spirit is full of love, that within you is the all-loving Self. Every day repeat to yourself the positive affirmation, "I am growing in love," and try to manifest that growing magnanimity of heart with the people around you. Think of sages and saints — how wonderful, loving, and kind they are. Then resolve to be like them and allow nothing to prevent you from attaining that goal.

By emphasizing positive traits, you cause the negative ones to gradually vanish. Even if they persist, it doesn't matter, because negativity does not have any substantiality. It is the positive that is your innate nature.

*Do It Now*

Do not procrastinate. Do what has to be done now! Procrastination is the greatest obstacle to greatness and success. Great ideas may come to everyone, but the difference between the people who succeed and those who do not depends on how quickly they act on their ideas. Successful people put their ideas into practice. The people who don't succeed are the ones who say, "Oh, I have a great idea, but maybe tomorrow I'll have a better one. Actually, I'll wait until I have many good ideas. Meanwhile I'll store my ideas in the computer until I'm ready to take up the project perfectly, without one single flaw." Well, that will never happen!

If, on a daily basis, you work with your ideas and projects, handling your responsibilities and tasks as they arise, you will get everything done, and with much less pressure. On the other hand, if you postpone things for the next day, thinking that you will have more time then, other things inevitably come up. Then your tasks multiply, pressure builds up, and you get so frustrated that when you look at your cluttered desk you're tempted to throw everything away and do nothing.

When you attend to things as they come, your mind remains relaxed and uncluttered and your mental energy is free to be used for attaining internal fulfillment. However, when you are constantly pressured by time because you have not done what you should have done, there is no room within your cluttered mental space for peace and relaxation.

Therefore, remember, "D-I-N": Do it now! Never postpone until later what can be done now! Act on your good ideas now! Do not wait even one day!

*Target*

One must always have a target, a goal towards which to strive. Professional and social goals should always be kept in view. Whatever you want to become, be it a successful scientist, a politician, or a religious person, strive to attain that goal. Never lose sight of the most important target — your spiritual target — Liberation. To be united with God is the ultimate goal of all studies.

Always remember with sincerity and determination what being a "S-T-U-D-E-N-T" implies:

S — STUDY
T — TENACITY
U — UNDERSTANDING
D — DEVOTION
E — ERADICATION OF DEFECTS
N — NOW
T — TARGET

If you remember this day by day, your experience as a student of life will be fulfilling and rewarding and you will attain all the goals you have set before you.

# VII

# Guidelines for Right Living

by Swami Ishwarananda

*[The following questions were submitted to Swami Ishwarananda of Chinmaya Mission, Los Angeles, who gives us a fresh interpretation of the scriptures as they apply to contemporary issues.]*

*Student Life:*

Q: How can students have respect for teachers and parents when many of these educators do not live a value-based life?

A: It is essential that elders live the values before they preach them to others. Honest living with conviction has to be attempted by these educators before they pass them on to the next generation. Yet, an intelligent student should realize the importance of values in his or her life, even if the teachers or parents do not practice them. Values add value to one's life; they are the foundation for true saintliness and success in life.

Q: The dating norm in Western culture is so different. Should young people be dating?

A: Dating is a method used in today's world so that people can get to know each other. However, they should understand that when meeting for a date they are trying to impress each other through gestures, sweet talk, gifts, and other ways, and it is only while sharing the many emotional and challenging situations in life that one shows one's true colors. Youth should be cautioned not to let dating end up too quickly in a physical relationship unless they are both ready to take responsibility for their actions.

*Family Life*

Q: What is the Hindu moral stand on a) interracial marriages b) arranged marriages?

A: From a cultural standpoint we face many challenges if we enter into an interracial marriage, for our outlook on life and many related responses to relationships are different in various cultures. If one has to adjust to the other in every situation, one's entire life becomes a continuous struggle and later on it would become even more of a challenge while raising children. While moral values more or less remain the same in all faiths, one should think about the cultural identity of one's own offspring before entering into such marital commitment.

Arranged marriages are equally challenging if the partners are not ready to accommodate each other in spite of their differences. Just by looking at the horoscope of an individual does not mean that we can fully understand the character and behavior of an individual. Maturity comes from proper upbringing, education, and devotion to God. Therefore the moral standard of the family should be kept in mind while choosing an appropriate partner for life.

Marriage is a mutual agreement to sacrifice for each other in order to achieve harmony and peace. It is commitment and not mere convenience. When this sacrifice is born of love and respect for each other it is noble and moral. If it is for economic and social convenience it may soon result in misunderstanding and conflicts.

Q: Certain issues that were considered to be wrong seem to be becoming the norm now. What is the Hindu moral stand on a) sex before marriage, b) abortion, c) homosexuality?

A: Mutual attraction begins at a very early age for both men and women. Physical changes take place as per nature's course. Therefore early education should help provide the required maturity so that children understand that sex is for procreation and not for casual pleasure and that such pleasure also brings responsibility with it. It is a sacred act to be performed later in life with the right partner in the construct of marriage.

Abortion is a sin unless it is proven that conception took place unwillingly. In today's society abortion on humanitarian grounds is accepted, thereby bringing relief to women who have become victims of deceit. However, if one has willingly entered into a physical relationship, which has resulted in a pregnancy, then abortion is morally wrong. With any independent act there is an underlying responsibility and that holds true for sexual activity too. In the Hindu scriptures (*śāstra*) it is clearly stated that sex is not considered a vehicle for entertainment but a sacred act for procreation and maintaining the race. However, sex within the confines of marriage is not harmful if it is not used in excess.

According to our scriptures, sex is meant for procreation therefore there is no mention of any other type of sexual activity such as homosexuality.

Q: Can one combine being a good parent with a full-time career?

A: First, find out what is important in life. It is love that builds relationships not money. If one believes that money can buy love from children, one would eventually face disappointments in life. Spending quality time with children will give them a strong foundation. It is no doubt a challenge for today's micro-families to combine careers with parenting. However, when one discovers that the growth of the child is hampered due to one's narrow and selfish priorities, one should sacrifice the material comfort for the sake of moral responsibility.

Q: Is divorce justified? And if so under what circumstances?

A: The Laws of Manu permit divorce. According to *Narad*

*Dharma Sūtra* (XII:92-100) and Laws of Manu (IX:76-81), divorce is permitted for a man as well as for a woman based on different grounds. A waiting period of one to eight years is normally required.

Q: The role of husband and wife differ, yet they are both equally important, please comment?

A: Even in commercial organizations everyone's role is different yet all work together for a common goal. Similarly, in a family the role of husband and wife differ. And if there is no common goal there will be lot of conflicts. Love along with devotion to God will work like magic in integrating family members. Devotion to God should be expressed in fulfilling the needs of the partner. In the marital relationship the beginning years are crucial since they help build the required trust and confidence in each other.

Q: Usually it is thought that the female should be more passive, is that true and why?

A: Mothers are always considered as loving beings, and fathers are considered to be responsible. Love and responsibility go hand in hand. Goodness is any day superior to being right. A passive attitude is not necessarily a weakness; it is a readiness to forgive unconscious errors and mistakes. And the heart of a mother naturally possesses this quality. It is because of this that forgiveness should become a choice-less option in a family unit! But in a social setup we cannot fully adhere to forgiveness as a social principle because the unscrupulous may misuse it.

Q: How can we balance our spiritual growth with a career in this competitive world?

A: Spiritual growth does not contradict our social life. The first step in spiritual growth demands adherence to *dharma* from every individual. It is competition that breeds comparison. If we can understand our own *dharma* and abide in it what is the need to compare oneself with another? The world does not care for the spiritual growth of any individual. It is therefore our own sensible thinking that would urge us to take up spiritual growth as a serious pursuit in life.

Q: How can we be good parents?

A: Teach goodness and morality, and live by what you teach. Children should learn to love and respect each other just by imitating their parents. Only a well-nurtured plant can give delightful fruits to everyone. Values begin at home and then spread to the society. Someone rightly said, "What you want to hear from the lips of your child, should come from you first." Teach them the following principles:

Value of time
Pleasure of working
Worth of character
Power of kindness
Influence of example
Virtue of patience
Dignity of simplicity
Impact of perseverance
Wisdom of economy
Thrill of originality

Q: If the wife or husband wants to become celibate and the partner does not, what is the responsibility toward the spouse?

A: To follow celibacy should be an outcome of desire for spiritual enlightenment and not a mere denial of a spouse's interest. Educate the spouse through persuasion. The danger of miscommunication will result in a spouse's superficial disinterest and distrust. One cannot spiritually progress if there is constant conflict in family life.

Q: Can one be married and be a *saṁnyāsī* or does one have to live in a forest?

A: Swami Tapovanam observed: "A householder should not behave like a *saṁnyāsī*, nor should a *saṁnyāsī* live like a householder." Fulfilling the responsibilities of a householder is imperative to move to the next stage in life. It is detachment that marks an ascetic life and one should not detach oneself from worldly ties until it happens in the mind of one's own accord. Will one ever be truly free if the mind finds pleasure in the worldly matters?

*Forest Life and Renunciation*

Q: Are these two stages still relevant in society today and if so, why? How do we go about living them today?

A: Forest life is a life of withdrawal from worldly matters. But one cannot abruptly end one's social life therefore preparation is necessary in order to slow down. Study of the scriptures and quiet contemplation should become a big part of daily life. Engage in family affairs only when necessary. Spend time in keeping good health and have a quiet mind. Engage in *satsanga* and selfless service, and consider all situations in life as ordained by the Supreme Lord. When the mind finds peace without engaging in the affairs of the world, the thoughts will naturally be directed towards the Self. Tolerate imperfections that you see all around you.

A man of renunciation should not judge the world. Let him engage in work related to divine knowledge and scriptural wisdom. The Laws of Manu (Ch. VI) say, "Let him patiently bear hard words, let him not insult anybody, and let him not become anybody's enemy for the sake of his body. Against an angry man let him not in return show anger, let him bless when he is cursed, and let him not utter speech devoid of truth. By the restraint of his senses, by the destruction of [the pairs of opposites] love and hatred; and by the abstention from injuring the creatures, he becomes fit for immortality."

Q: What are we retiring from?

A: Retiring from the mind is a challenge that every spiritual aspirant will have to face. We cannot renounce *vāsanās* or tendencies unless we rise above the worldly habits that strengthen them. Retire from pleasures, and resolve to find peace within.

Q: If one partner is more inclined toward spiritual practice would he or she be justified in leaving their spouse to further their own spiritual growth?

A: With the permission of the spouse, one can embrace renunciation, but not otherwise. In *Bṛhadāraṇyaka Upaniṣad* (II:4.1-3) we find such an occasion in the life of Yajnavalkya.

He said to his wife, "Maitreyi, I am resolved to renounce the world and begin the life of renunciation. I wish therefore to divide my property between you and my other wife, Katyayani."

Maitreyi replied: "My Lord, if this whole earth belonged to me with all its wealth, should I through its possession attain immortality?"

Yajnavalkya said, "No. Your life would be like that of the rich. None can possibly hope to attain immortality through wealth."

Maitreyi replies, "Then what need have I of wealth? Please, my Lord, tell me what do you know about the way to immortality?"

Yajnavalkya eventually initiated his wife into Self-knowledge. However, it is not justified to leave behind children who have not yet reached their adulthood, or to leave without the consent of the spouse. For example, the well known Maratha saint, Shri Gyanadev's father, Vitthalpanth, returned to the life of a householder after embracing renunciation.

Q: Should retired couples help raise their grandchildren while the parents are on a career path?

A: In the world today where both parents have to work to meet the financial needs of the comfort–driven family, it is better to leave the children in the care of parents who are retired rather than babysitters. While taking care of the children they can engage in self-study, prayers, and also teach values through stories to the young minds. Identification with the elders of the family enables the children to become more in touch with the original flavor of their culture. They can even observe and absorb the ways to treat the elders of the family from their own parents.

Q: What is the Hindu moral stand on euthanasia?

A: If one believes in the law of karma, which is one of the fundamental tenets of *Sanātana Dharma*, then the practice of euthanasia will be in conflict with such faith. The process of death is described in *Bṛhadāraṇyaka Upaniṣad* (IV:4.2): "All organs detaching themselves from his physical body, unite with his subtle body. Then the light of the Self lights the point of his heart, where the nerves join, and by that light he departs either through the eye, or through the gate of the skull, or through some other aperture of the body. When he thus departs, life departs; and when life departs, all the functions of the vital principle depart. The self (soul) remains conscious, and the dying man goes to his abode. The deeds of this life, and the impressions they leave behind, follow him." Thus forcing death will be against the natural process of soul's exit. Therefore, euthanasia can be regarded appropriate or inappropriate based only on the faith of the person concerned.

# PART THREE

# *Family Life*

*The householder's renunciation,*
*when it is at the altar of their love for Thee,*
*also delivers liberation to them.*
*Not by wearing external saṁnyāsa dress*
*or by going on pilgrimages*
*or by having the yati-mark*
*can one attain freedom of personality.*

*Swami Tapovanam*
*Hymn to Ganga*

The widest possibilities for spiritual growth lie in the give-and-take of everyday relationships. The truth of this is brought out sweetly in a story about Saint Francis of Assisi. Three young men approached Francis and asked his blessing to become hermits and seek God each in his own cave, deep in the mountains of Umbria. Francis smiled. He instructed them to be hermits indeed, but hermits all together in a single hut. One should take the role of father; a second should think of himself as the mother, and the third should be their child. Every few months they should exchange roles.

Living in this way they were to establish among themselves perfect harmony, thinking always of the needs of one another. We can almost see the three would-be recluses exchanging sidelong glances. Their teacher had issued them a greater challenge than any they had bargained for. Yet they carried out Francis's instructions, discovering that human relationships are the perfect tool for sanding away our rough edges and getting at the core of divinity within us. We need look no further than our own family, friends, acquaintances, or even adversaries to begin our practice.

Eknath Easwaran

# VIII

# Advice to Householders

## by Swami Chinmayananda

Q: How do we deal with the constant challenges in daily life?

A: Life is spent in meeting challenges. Situations and problems continuously flow toward us; we do not have to look for them. But how we deal with them is what matters, and to meet them efficiently is the game. Sometimes we win, sometimes we lose, but meet them we must. There is no choice. If we meet them with courage and faith in ourselves we win, but if we are not dynamic and diligent all the time they will crush us. This is the law-of-life. It becomes a sport, no doubt exhausting, but exhilarating at the same time. We can enjoy it all only if we take it as a life-long sport. In order to be a good player, however, we must have a mind full of reserve energy and inexhaustible inner stamina. An exhausted and fatigued mind becomes affected by situations, crushed by problems, and tortured by life. It is not that life has the strength to persecute us, but we are too weak and thus we allow life to play havoc with us.

Be strong, not merely with the physical strength of a bull, but the subtle vitality of a calm mind, diligent in its application, consistent in its logical thinking, and replete with a will to win over all negative tendencies that poison and weaken the mind. "Be yourself" is the simple motto of right living. Weaknesses are not ours; rise above them. Above the level of both good and bad, illuminating both equally and not getting in any way contaminated by them (like the sun lighting up both the ugly and the beautiful) resides the Inner Essence "That Thou Art." This inner ruling factor is God. This Essence of life is the true You. All the sorrow and pains, losses and gains belong to the body and not the true You, this is the *Ātman* of the *Vedāntin*.

Life is not and should not be one constant steady flow; and when you see dark clouds gathering and storms threatening you need not despair and leave the boat. Be steady at the helm of Truth and steer toward the safer path, which the rishis chalked out. Constantly refer to the compass of inner purity, gaze self-ward, and proceed full speed. Keep smiling. Accept adverse criticism. Do not get perturbed. Words are but disturbances in the air created by merely moving the tongue. If there is nothing true in the criticism, ignore it all as meaningless chatter. If there is truth in it, accept it with gratitude and bring about the necessary changes in yourself. Thus improve and come to shine more than ever before, and be grateful to all your creative critics.

Q: How do we know what our duties are? How can we perform them correctly?

A: To perform and fulfill your duties correctly you must carefully reflect and understand your place in the society. As an individual you have duties toward yourself. As a domestic being you have duties toward your family members. As a social being you have duties toward the society, and lastly, as a member in a competitive world you have some duties toward your chosen profession. All these duties are to be undertaken and fulfilled with a sense of loyalty and devotion to the Lord who in His great wisdom has placed you exactly where you are supposed to be. Your duties toward the elderly do not just extend to the home, but toward all older citizens around you. The present is the product of the past. The older generation carved out the present, for better or worse. And now you have been given an opportunity to serve them in their old age. If everyone looks after their parents and their children the society will be vigorous and secure. But this is not usually the case because of our indifference, which is born out of selfishness. In a blind search for our personal happiness we ignore and refuse this duty. Children become neglected, and teenagers run wild with no clear goal in life. Morality goes and everyone becomes confused.

Q: What are the duties that we have toward ourselves?

A: The duty that we have toward ourselves is to live in self-control, to eat and sleep properly, to exercise, and to maintain a loving and peaceful attitude toward all. Gain spiritual knowledge so that you can serve the people around you in the proper way. Never give up self-study, worship the Lord, and meditate regularly. Say your daily prayers even if you are traveling or are not well. This alone can bring sweetness into your life. This alone is the path of spirituality.

Q: I always read that attachments are bad — either to things or to people — and yet how is it possible to live with the family members all our lives and not get attached to them? If we keep an animal in the house for a few days we even get attached to it, so how is it possible not to get attached to affectionate, considerate, and friendly human beings?

A: You are unfortunately misunderstanding the exact meaning of the terms "attachment" and "love." When we come to depend upon things and beings for our sense of security and fullness it becomes attachment; attachment shackles and makes us prisoners. Love, however, is an expansion of ourselves. In our identification with all things and beings, we embrace everyone. Then we do not need them for our fullness and therefore we are free. Love liberates our mind. Attachment compels us to be slaves to the world, and we feel shattered without those beings and things. When the mind feels pressured to think, "I cannot live without it," it becomes attachment. In short, ego plus selfish desire is attachment.

Q: How can a householder learn to control his mind and body so that he can be ready for a higher step? Is there a precise method?

A: The path is the same whether one is a householder or a renunciate. As long as our attention is with the body, we discover a hundred excuses to run into the world of objects seeking gratification. But when the mind becomes attached to an inspiring goal or ideal, its nature changes and its attention turns toward the Higher. When your child is playing with your new silver-plated pen, the only way to persuade the child to give it up is to offer him a piece of chocolate.

In a householder's life, total abstinence is not allowed. But overindulgence, all excesses such as overeating, overworking, over-anxiety, over-ambition must be curtailed, including over-exerting and oversleeping. Prayer in the morning and in the evening and daily reading of at least a few pages of inspiring spiritual literature should be a helpful program for both husband and wife. If you still find your mind difficult to control on a given day, take only fruit that day, but do not make it a habit, and take to this diet only when you feel that your mind is out of control.

Q: How can we learn to act without selfish motives?

A: If we fix our vision high and act with a spirit of surrender and dedication the mind becomes purified, and the *vāsanās* (inner tendencies, impressions) automatically exhaust themselves. If we can learn to act without selfish, desire-prompted motives we can grow to unbelievable heights wherever we are. This is what is meant by *niṣkāma karma*.

Unwinding the *vāsanās* is the spiritual practice by which the ego rediscovers for itself its own essential nature of freedom and peace. This unwinding of the *vāsanās* cannot be successfully undertaken merely through meditation at a fixed period of time during the day. Unless we are careful in our contacts with the world, at our body, mind, and intellect levels the unwinding cannot be completely successful. Through meditation, no doubt, the subtle *vāsanās* are wiped out, but the grosser ones can be loosened and removed only in the fields of activity where we have gathered them. Hence *niṣkāma karma* is absolutely unavoidable. Detachment is easily interpreted as indifference. But there is a big difference between indifference and detachment. Indifference cannot bring forth our spiritual blossoming. Detachment from the world does not mean that we should not perceive forms, sounds, tastes, touch, or smell. As long as we have the five sense organs, the sense objects must impinge upon us. But the aftermath of this mental reception of the external stimuli is what confuses us.

Lord Buddha was once insulted. He quietly stood and listened, and when the insulter had finished, Lord Buddha quietly walked out. The disciple following him was surprised, and the Lord's answer to the boy is a good example of detachment. The Lord of Compassion said, "My boy, he *gave* me insults; but I did not *receive* them; naturally these insults are with the very person who gave it to me; if you have received them you may go and return them, but I have not received them." Buddha heard the sound of the words, but he did not bring his ego to play upon them and think about the consequences. Fancied imaginations spun by an uncontrolled mind at the impulses received from stimuli of the outer world are called *karma phala* (consequences of action). To detach from the fruits of actions is the real detachment.

Q: I have studied the scriptures for many years, yet I do not experience peace and harmony in my life. Please comment.

A: The human mind stands between two worlds: The upper world of harmony and the lower world of discord and chaos. To the extent we withdraw ourselves from the clamor of the lower and tune ourselves up to the sweet music of the higher, to that extent we are spiritual and divine. Whatever the methods by which this is achieved are all considered methods of religion. Yet we become truly spiritual, not by rotating prayer beads, or reading books, and not by merely singing the glory of the Lord, but by sincerely living in tune with the higher and nobler in ourselves.

It is a divine sign of the grace of the Lord that we are made to feel impatient with a mere intellectual appreciation of the scriptures. There must be a continuous thirst for experiencing the truths in our own subjective life. This is not too difficult. If sincere in seeking, and regular in practice, the experience can be with us. There is no doubt about it. No past or present circumstance can be a real bar to it. Removal of what veils our divine nature is what is to be accomplished in spiritual life. Carry the mental mood of sanctified purity as far as possible at all occasions and in all your fields of activities. This can be done with a little conscious and sincere effort. You will see a new glow of success and derive much satisfaction from whatever work that you are now doing.

Q: All around me I see people suffer, how can I be most effective in trying to help the society?

A: Your empathy for the suffering of people shows that you have a noble loving heart. This is an essential factor in the composition of any true spiritual seeker. But it becomes ineffective when it is not supported by some strength and capacity in yourself. This dynamism comes out of your own spiritual growth. Without that growth any attempt on our part to give happiness to others can bring only general confusion and perhaps more sorrow. This is what we are experiencing now in the world.

If I want to be charitable and put my hands mechanically into my pocket and there is nothing in my pocket, yet I try to empty it into the bowls of the beggars, I will not be relieving them of their sorrow, no matter how often I may repeat this idle movement. Similarly, when we do not have the purity, peace, and perfection within ourselves, the world will not be redeemed by our activities. Perhaps we may relieve the world of one sorrow, by providing them with another! If Elephantiasis transferred from my right leg to my left leg can be considered as a cure, then every new social order can be considered as a relief measure. Remember true spiritual workers also have the highest regard for the world and the greatest sympathy for its sorrows. However, their methods are to bring to the community of men a more enduring peace and a more satisfying joy by teaching them about spiritual values.

Q: What is the best kind of food for a spiritual student?

A: The spiritual student has to cultivate a subtle intellect, and since the materials that we receive through food determines our mental constitution, the spiritual student should take only *sāttvika* food and avoid food which goes to nourish *rājasika* and *tāmasika* tendencies. [see pages 103 for discussion on food group] Eat only foods that are easily digestible. Do not overeat, and eat sparingly at night.

I would like to warn you against any fanaticism in regard to food habits however. Religion is not a matter of the kitchen. More important than external purification is inner purification, control of the passions and so on. Remember what Ramakrishna Paramahamsa said, "If a man loves God, living upon the flesh of a pig, he is blessed. But wretched is the person who lives on milk and rice but whose mind is absorbed in lust and gold."

Q: Could you give some guidelines as to how to work with less stress?

A: Problems become manageable only when the mind is calm. Years ago in the U.S. around the 1930's the newspapers talked of social and political situations. Then around the 1940's, those situations had turned into problems. By the fifties and sixties, the words "situation" and "problem" had disappeared from our vocabulary, and everything had become a crisis. Now all we read about in the papers is the education crisis, the health crisis, and the oil crisis. Nothing has really changed about the situations in the world, but we have a reduced capacity to deal with them. We need to develop that capacity of the mind to cope. If you treat a given event as a situation, it is just a situation to be dealt with. Keeping your mind calm, don't let the situation grow into a problem, and then develop further into a crisis.

Q: How can I overcome feelings of loneliness?

A: Understand the difference between being lonely and living alone. Once when I was in college, a wealthy man gave me the key to his house, which was built upon a hill and was the only house for miles around. The family had gone somewhere and they told me I could stay there all by myself to prepare for my examination. I moved into the house and was really happy until the evening. After all the servants had left for the day in that big house with no one near for miles around, I felt very unhappy as I was quite lonely.

Later on when I was in Uttarkashi I was in my cottage all by myself with no one around, yet I was not afraid nor unhappy. When you are alone, you are alone with the Lord. But when your thoughts are not with the Lord, you will feel lonely, and no one likes to feel lonely. Loneliness is painful, but to be alone with the Lord in your thoughts is the ideal way to live. To be a *saṁnyāsin* means to live alone with the Lord as your heart's companion.

## Spiritual Education for Children

Q: We have two children, both under three years of age. How do we actively begin our children's spiritual education beyond what they passively learn by observing their parents, so that their spiritual progress may be constant, subtle, and consistent?

A: Do not ever misunderstand that children of that age are merely passive observers. In fact, only after we have grown up do we learn the art of passive, dull, sleepy, and sloppy observation, if children of that age are passive observers, how then are they able to learn a language? Is not everything new, fresh, and mysterious for them? In fact, child psychologists have concluded that children in that age group need more rest as well as more frequent feedings because during those few years of early childhood they have to be alert and learn much more than in their later life. The rate of absorption of knowledge and experiences in those early years is stupendous. Therefore, an atmosphere of religion and spiritual values around them is very important in molding and enhancing their mental life.

Between the ages of three and five, your children can be introduced to stories of Christ and Krishna, of Rama and Buddha, and of Mohammed and Moses. These stories of the spiritual giants of the world, recounting their experiences, their trials and inner strength in overcoming temptations, as well as the positive experiences of joy that they gained, may all be passed on to your children with appropriate expressiveness.

Let these stories be told now and then by the father also. Make it a point for the children to pray before their meals, not too elaborately, but for just a short moment. Whenever they ask questions about flowers, clouds, butterflies, or frogs be alert enough to flavor your honest explanations with a hint about the play of God around us. Leave them with these small hints. Do not go into details. Allow a corner in your home for prayer — a quiet private chapel or simple altar. Let your children watch both of you praying to the Lord regularly.

When the children have grown to be between the ages of eight and ten, at a fixed time for one half hour every day, sit down with them and read them *The Gospel of Shri Ramakrishna*. I suggest this book because much is expressed in the innocent language of children. The endless stories and analogies can lead their minds on an independent journey to see for themselves a greater message for life and a larger value in life.

Q: May I know what you mean by yoga for children?

A: I do not recommend any yoga for children. All they need is perhaps *sūrya namaskār* (a series of physical movements called "salutation to the sun"), stories from the *Purāṇa* (mystical stories), and stories of great devotees, so that they will gather the higher values of life and have a mental image of their heroes. It would be criminal to give them postures *āsanas* and breathing exercises *praṇāyāma*. In their enthusiasm they would overdo it, and competent guidance in this particular field is rare.

Q: What can we do to bring about a brighter world for our children to grow in?

A: If the future is to be bright we have to mold our children to think in a new pattern and with a new vision. It is a slow process. It is not a revolution, but it is the evolution of each individual character. We cannot gain this understanding through some revised textbook or because there is a lot of talk in the media about value-based educational systems. Mere talk is not sufficient. We, the parents, must change. Children do not learn from books. These higher values cannot be imparted to the students by institutions, a society, a community, or even a committee. Children imitate their parents. It is the mother at home who gives values and ideals to the child and molds the mental thinking of the child. Only when a plant is young and we are sincerely watching it, can we train the plant to grow straight. A plant can be trained but not a tree.

Similarly, training of our children can only be done between the ages of six and twelve, a little more can be done up to the age of eighteen, but after that the tree becomes set. Then one has to go through fire in order to become plastic enough to change. Once we have gone beyond the younger years, it is not so easy to change our pattern of thoughts, our angle of vision, and our attitude to things and beings. So early childhood is the time for training and mothers are mainly responsible. It is the mother alone who imparts the tender emotions and values, who lives the ideals of charity, goodness, tenderness, affection, and forgiveness. The mother demonstrates these ideals in her life, she never gives a discourse as the father would. The children see it and so these ideas become embedded in them. When mothers lose touch with their spiritual values all the children will be effected. When these same children become youngsters they start looking around and they find that the values that have been given to them are all hollow and empty. They don't feel satisfied, but they dare not fight with the system around them. They want to escape, and they usually escape through alcohol or drugs.

It is time, therefore, that mothers learn the cultural values of the country, for the sake of the children and the future. We must teach the children not only to have right values and convictions of their own but also to have the heroism to live up to them. If we can impart that kind of training to only one child, we will ensure a better future for ourselves. We are neglecting our children unconsciously, and in our thoughtlessness or lack of correctly viewing things we have become only machines to produce children. We have to take responsibility for molding and beautifying our children, prepare them to face the world of tomorrow and to lead and guide the world of the future. It is a tremendous responsibility. Once we realize the responsibility we will be handling our children much more intelligently.

Even animals and birds train their children properly. Is there a bird that has neglected its young and not taught them how to balance on their wings? The mother spends time on training them. It is only among intelligent human beings that the parents neglect their children.

The remedy is with us. We are not giving enough respect, reverence, or true affection to our children. Once these values come back, nature herself will guide every mother in how to train the children.

# IX

# *Parenting*

*by Swami Tejomayananda*

The first requirement when facing any problem in life, whether it is in the family or at work, is to keep the mind calm and relaxed. At the same time we need to understand that the problems that we are facing are not unique. For example, when we become ill we think that the doctor must see us immediately, but the doctor does not get excited because he or she is used to seeing many such cases daily. Whatever problems we may have, we need to realize that they are all just a part of life, and the same applies to the problems of parenting. Whenever our children are misbehaving we need to reflect on our own childhood and especially our teenage years. Every intelligent person rebels while growing up, some of us may have rebelled at the mental level and some physically; and some of us may have even run away from home. But now that we are raising our own children we seem to have forgotten all that. The issues and concerns that we face today with regard to raising children are nothing new, they were also there in the days of Socrates and as far back as the *Purāṇa*. The Greek philosopher Socrates, who lived from 470-399 B.C., was known to have commented on the disobediance of children. So the situations that we face today may be different but the fundamental problem of humankind remains the same.

# SWAMI TEJOMAYANANDA

## *The Problem of I-ness*

When we say "children" are we really worried about *all* children, or only our children? Let us look at it from the highest spiritual standpoint. When we think a little more deeply we will realize that our anxiety is not for children in general, but it is for *my* child. Therefore the problem is not in the child, but with our idea of "my-ness." And when we go a step further we realize that the action of my child has a direct bearing on me, and on my image. If our children behave well we want everyone to know that it is our child, but when they misbehave we don't want anyone to know. When the children are smart the parents will say that it is in their genes, but when children become uncontrollable some parents will even disown their own children. Thus from the spiritual standpoint, all the worry and anxiety comes from the sense of "I-ness" and "My-ness." When we look at it objectively we will discover that what really upsets us is a concern for our own image.

The following personal example will illustrate this: In 1981, Swami Chinmayananda, my guru, told me that I had to conduct the Vedanta training course in Sidhabari for the first time in Hindi. Upon receiving the applications, the person in charge told me that the candidates did not appear to be all that good. After listening to his comments I wondered why I was getting upset since I had not even seen the applications, let alone the candidates. Then it occurred to me that this course was the first of its kind to be offered by Chinmaya Mission in Hindi, and that I was the one who would be teaching it. If the students did not turn out well, everyone would want to know who had taught them. So it was the "I" thought that had caused me to be upset. But the moment I realized that if they were inspired from within, the Lord would automatically bring them, I was able to relax completely. That very first group produced some brilliant students, many of them were highly educated, and all those students are now doing wonderful work. So we can see that it is the "I" that is the cause of all worry.

## Everyone Belongs to God

Vedanta encourages us to ask the question, "Are we this physical body?" When parents say, "I gave birth to this child," the question arises as to what exactly was born of the parents. The parents are only the suppliers of the material of the physical body for that individual to live in. But the parents did not create that individual. Moreover the parents do not have the faintest idea as to how that physical body is made. Not even the mother knows exactly what happens in her womb. So what are we taking credit for? When we begin to reflect deeply on these matters then the notion of "I-ness" and the sense of doership will gradually disappear. It is a false notion to think that we are taking care of the child. Who took care of the child in the womb? The One who took care of the child then, will take care later on as well. We seem to have an erroneous notion that we are doing something.

From the Vedantic standpoint every individual belongs to God. As parents we only provide the material for the physical body of that person. An individual *jīva*, or soul, comes into this world along with certain tendencies to fulfill a purpose. As members of a family they are all placed together, but everyone has come for a different reason. For example, when we travel by plane or train we do not know who our co-passengers will be. But all the passengers have a common karma; all of them wanted to travel on that day and at that time. However, if you ask them individually where they are going and why, everyone will have a different answer.

Similarly, in a family there has to be some kind of common karma for all of the members to have come together in one place, though the purpose for each may be different. We may spend some time together sharing good times and bad, and then like fellow travelers we get off at various places and go our own separate ways. The famous poet, Kahlil Gibran, says in *The Prophet* that the children come through you, they don't belong to you, like the arrow that comes through the bow but does not belong to that bow; it just follows its own course.

Lord Krishna says in the *Bhagavad Gītā*: "I am the Father of this world, the Mother, the supporter and the grandsire: the One to be known, the Purifier, OM (the syllable), and also the *Ṛg*, the *Sama* and the *Yajur.*" (IX:17)

Thus the Lord Himself clearly declares that He is the Mother, the Father, and the Grandfather of this universe. Why then do you as parents think that you have become the mother and father? When we conduct our Vedanta training course, many people ask me how the students are shaping up. I tell them that I can never judge ahead of time because sometimes we think that a certain brilliant student is doing very well, and then he suddenly quits the course. On the other hand, a student whom we may have thought was not fit for the course may turn out to be the very best in his class. It is very strange. Why should we judge? Let the Lord alone judge.

### Our Role

Our role should be rooted in the fact that we belong to God, and that we are all instruments in the hands of the Lord. The Lord is so great that He wants to give everyone credit and an opportunity to achieve. In the *Bhagavad Gītā* it is said: "Therefore, stand up and obtain fame. Conquer the enemies and enjoy the flourishing kingdom. Verily by Myself they have already been slain, be you a mere instrument, O left-handed archer." (XI: 33)

Each of us is a part of the Lord, and the Lord of the universe is the real Mother and Father. Swami Ramdas said that there is one nature *prakṛti* and then there is the Lord *Paramātman*. Where did the third entity "I" come from? It is this "I" that is a thief. Our role is only that of an instrument. We are not the doer, but an instrument of doing. The real doer is the Lord. The first verse in *Upadeśa Sāra* says: "By the command of the Creator of the world, the fruits of action are gained. When the Lord, the doer (*Jagat Kartā*) is there, what can this "I" do?" So we have seen that the Lord has given the parents a chance to bring up a child, but they need to remember that this child belongs to the Lord and that they also belong to Him.

Gurudev, Swami Chinmayananda, used to say that our role is like that of a farmer or a gardener. We do not create the seed or the soil. The potential power is already in the seed. The role of a farmer, an agriculturist, or a gardener is to prepare the soil properly, then to sow the seeds at the right time, and to give them the required amount of water, shade, and sunlight. In short, this will provide a conducive environment for the seeds to grow. If the seeds have something in them, they will sprout. But if the seeds themselves are roasted then what can the gardener do? Therefore, in the first place, the seed has to have the potential power to grow into something. Our effort is only one of the contributory factors. It is the totality of this world that really acts on the seed. Therefore remember that the result of our efforts, the *karma phala*, does not come because of our karma alone. Our duty is to provide the right atmosphere in given situations. If we have made all the appropriate efforts and the expected results still do not come, then we are not to be blamed. Our conscience will be clear that we did our very best. This not only applies to parenting, but to every activity in life.

As parents our job is to give our children food, clothing, shelter, and education. Along with education, we also have to give them good culture, namely, the foundation of good habits (*samskāra*). Many times parents want culture for their children and they send them to our classes for youth called "Bala Vihar," while they themselves watch TV. They think that since they come from India they already know all about it, but the fact is that many of the parents are no longer that familiar with their own culture. One of the reasons we conduct family spiritual camps is to nurture an environment where the family can grow together. If we want the children to be cultured, we also have to follow the same rules. Teaching values and culture to our children should start even before the child is born because the child starts learning while he or she is in the mother's womb. That is the rationale behind prenatal education, and our scriptures also confirm this. That is why Swami Chinmayananda used to say that "Culture cannot be taught, it can only be caught."

If we want our children to be bright, cultured, and disciplined we will have to start by developing the same qualities in ourselves. In the *Bhagavad Gītā* it is clearly said: "Whatever a great man does, that other men also do; whatever he sets as the standard, that the world follows." (III:21) We need to prepare ourselves properly for the job of parenting. Remember how much we needed to prepare before our annual examination? Even now we go to great lengths to prepare for a job interview, yet when it comes to living our entire life, there is no preparation. The main reason why life seems to be a problem is because we are not adequately prepared for it. And in order to prepare for life we need scriptural teachings from spiritual teachers.

*Look for the Cause*

In the human body whenever there is an infection or disease, the body shows some symptoms. There are exceptions, such as cancer that does not show any symptom for a long time and therefore goes undetected. But generally there are some symptoms such as pain, and these symptoms really are a blessing. In the same way, with reference to parenting, we need to become sensitive to our children's reactions. If a child suddenly begins to behave in a peculiar manner, we must try to discover the reason. There has to be a reason, because without a cause there is no effect. One of the reasons could be that the child is just following the growth pattern. Certain physical changes take place in their bodies while they go through the various stages of childhood and teenage years. At the same time mental changes take place as all the tendencies (*vāsanā*) that were dormant earlier, also begin to manifest. And as I said before, we must remember that we also passed through similar stages. Sometimes we give undue importance to these changes and worry too much, but it is good to remember that it may only be a passing phase.

In this context let me give you a personal example. As a child, whenever my mother asked me to read religious books to her I used to do it quite willingly. Then there came a time when I stopped doing that. I not only refused to read the *Rāmāyaṇa* to her, but I also criticized it. I know it is hard to believe this because now I am giving so many discourses on *Rāmāyaṇa*.

My point here is that everybody goes through certain phases, but everyone outgrows this eventually. Children will have certain reactions because of their age, as well as the influence of their peers. Your children want to assert their individuality; they want to be independent. Why should they listen to someone, especially their parents? And why blame them? Understand them instead. We become upset because we have not thought deeply enough and have not yet gained a complete vision of life. We also do not see how our reactions tend to aggravate the problems. So become sensitive to the changes taking place in your children and be aware of their reactions. Find out the causes.

Those of us who have come from India have already been educated there, but our children were born and raised here. And this is why we must expect our children's perspective to be totally different from ours. The environment outside is different from the one at home. They are growing up in a dual atmosphere. We say that the children should remain totally unaffected, but this is not possible. The fact is that they will be affected by outside influences. Even the minds of great yogis and ascetics slip. Our job is only to give them a balanced view.

A great Sanskrit poet said, "Anything that is old does not mean it is gold!" In the same way everything new is not necessarily bad. Look at things objectively and then accept or reject them. *Rāmacarit Mānas* says it very beautifully: "This world is a mixture of sentient and insentient things and beings. It is a mixture of good and bad. It is like milk mixed with water. They say that the proverbial swan takes only the milk, and leaves the water. In the same way, the saints or the intelligent people take what is good and reject what is bad."

Therefore, we should try to teach the children to see what is good, and not get carried away by physical beauty. Teach your children to discriminate. To absorb whatever good they see, and to drop whatever they see as not being right. The same attitude should be applied with reference to India. Make sure that you do not give your children the idea of division, that is, whatever is in America is bad, and whatever is in India is good.

Parents also have to be aware to not give orders, sermons, or advice to their children. Make them feel that the ideas are coming from them and act as facilitators only. Corporations have a strategy of making their employees do what management wants them to do without making it appear like an order. This is called strategic administering. It is not easy, but the results are well worth it.

In every one of us there is a tendency to impose our ideas on others; all of us have a bit of a dictator in us. We may not be doing it consciously, but it happens. This tendency to impose our ideas is present in every human being in some measure. For example, some of us want to realize our unfulfilled dreams vicariously through our children; we still want to experience and enjoy certain achievements indirectly through them. Therefore, we have to be careful to see that we are not imposing our ideas on them.

Whenever we want another person to take an interest in what we are doing we first have to take an interest in them. Let me give you an example: I went to a home where the hosts were the parents of two sons. The parents encouraged their children to ask me anything. The children immediately replied that they did not have any questions. After breakfast I went to the boys' room and asked them to tell me about their hobbies. They told me that they loved baseball. So I asked them to teach me all about it. They became very enthusiastic and began to show me a video.

Slowly they began to ask their questions about religion and culture. This shows that when we take an interest in others, rapport is built. It is extremely important to establish a rapport between you and your children. In their hearts, there has to be love and total confidence in you. They must be able to confide in you, and have nothing to hide from you. When this kind of rapport is built, everything else becomes easy. Otherwise even minor things can be very irritating and disturbing.

Some parents have serious problems with their children. But remember that it has come to this stage only because certain situations were not taken care of earlier. We cannot go back in time, but even now we can start building the rapport. However, if you find that everything you do irritates the child, then you have to go through someone for whom the child has some regard. You should worry only if the child is into alcohol, drugs, or bad company such as organized gangs. Then your anxiety is justified.

### Develop the Right Vision

I have talked to your children, and they have told me that you expect too much of them and you want them to be first class in everything. Some of them would love to see your school records! I also wonder why you are constantly after them. Allow your children to grow at their own pace and let them do the things that they want to do while disciplining them slowly and gently. There are no magical solutions, but it is very helpful to have a complete vision of life.

In Sanskrit, there is a beautiful little verse about parenting that says, "Fondle your child up to the age of five, at that time treat him like a king or queen or God. Then the next ten years be strict with him, discipline him, and educate him. When they are sixteen years old treat them like your friend."

Strictness does not mean that you become cruel. Some children may not need any kind of disciplining, while others may require some. We do it the other way around, however. In the early years we just allow them to do whatever they want. And when they become sixteen, we treat them like a five-year-old. At that time they will naturally resent it and tell you that they are not children anymore. Then they become wild while the parents want them to be mild.

Many times children do certain things because of peer pressure and not because they *want* to do it. They talk about revolting against their parents, but they do not have the courage to revolt against peer pressure. So I ask them, "How come your independent spirit only comes up when dealing with your parents? Why doesn't that same independent spirit arise when you are with your friends? How come your friends succeed in pressuring you? Why can't you stand up and say that you are not going to do this?" Once they see the logic behind this they will begin to think along these lines themselves.

Sometimes people ask me how are we going to teach our values and our culture to our children while living in the West. But it can be done. Help them understand the difference between right and wrong and what will happen if they follow either path. Once they have been given the right vision and values are instilled in them, they will follow them with conviction and confidence.

I would like to summarize this talk by repeating the first statement: When dealing with the problems in life pertaining to your children, let your mind remain calm and relaxed. There is nothing to worry about unless the child is going to extremes. We have seen that the real cause of the problem is our sense of "I-ness," and "my-ness," as well as our expectations of them. Once you understand this concept, you will find successful ways and means to deal with different situations that may arise. In this entire process, always remember that *you belong to God.* Invoke God's blessings on yourself, your child, and on everyone. The inner controller is the Lord.

Perhaps you can pray along the following lines, "Oh Lord I

cannot change this person directly. I do not know what is happening to him. But you, Oh Lord, can do anything. So please shower your blessings on him. You are the inspirer of thoughts. So please inspire his mind." If you pray like this and become calm and quiet, things will change for the good. I would like to wish all your children a very bright future.

# X

## Daily Life As Meditation

### by Jack Kornfield

In expanding our circle of practice, we may feel that we haven't enough time. Modern life is already very fast-paced and getting more so all the time. Saving time is even beginning to replace sex as a means of selling products on television. Do we have enough time to expand our practice? Remember how someone complained to Achaan Chah that there wasn't enough time to practice in his monastery because there were so many chores — sweeping, cleaning, greeting visitors, building, chanting, and so forth — and Achaan Chah asked back, "Is there enough time to be aware?" Everything we do in life is a chance to awaken.

We can learn to see here and now those places where we are afraid or attached or lost or deluded. We can see in the very same moment the possibility of awakening, of freedom, of fullness of being. We can carry on this practice anywhere — at work, in our community, at home. Sometimes people complain about how difficult it is to practice in family life. When they were single, they could take long periods of silent retreats or spend time in the mountains or travel to exotic temples, and then these places and postures became confused in their mind with the spirit of the sacred itself. But the sacred is always here before us. Family life and children are a wonderful temple. Children can become fantastic teachers for us. They teach us surrender and selflessness. They bring us into the present moment again and again. When we're in an ashram or monastery, if our guru tells us to get up early in the morning to meditate, we may not always feel like it. Some mornings we may roll over and go back to sleep thinking we'll do it another day. But when our children awaken in the middle of the night because they are sick and need us, there's no choice and no question about it — we respond instantly with our entire loving attention.

Over and over we are asked to bring our whole heart and care to family life. These are the same instructions a meditation master or guru gives us when we face the inevitable tiredness, restlessness, or boredom in our meditation cell or temple. Facing these at home is no different from facing them in the meditation retreat. Spiritual life becomes more genuine when things become more difficult. Our children have inevitable accidents and illnesses. Tragedies occur. These situations call for a constancy of our love and wisdom. Through them we touch the marrow of practice and find our true spiritual strength.

In many other cultures the nurturing of wise and healthy children is seen as a spiritual act, and parenting is considered sacred. Children are held constantly, both physically and in the heart of the community, and each healthy child is seen as a potential Leonardo, Nureyev, Clara Barton, a unique contributor to humanity. Our children are our meditation. When children are raised by day care and television, in a society that values money-making more than its children, we create generations of discontented, wounded, needy individuals. A key to extending practice into the demanding areas of child rearing and intimate relationships is the same development of patience or constancy as in following our breath, bringing our heart back a thousand times. Nothing of value grows overnight, not our children, nor the capacity of our hearts to love one another. I saw the power that grows from loving respect on a family sabbatical to Thailand and Bali. My daughter Caroline studied Balinese dance for two months with a wonderful teacher, and when she finished he proposed to stage a farewell recital for her at his school, which is also his home. When we arrived they set out a stage, got the music ready, and then started to dress Caroline. They took a very long time dressing a six-year-old whose average attention span is about five minutes. First they draped her in a silk sarong, with a beautiful chain around her waist. Then they wrapped embroidered silk fifteen times around her chest. They put on gold armbands and bracelets. They arranged her hair and put a golden flower in it. They put on more makeup than a six-year-old girl could dream of.

Meanwhile I sat there getting impatient, the proud father eager to take pictures. "When are they going to finish dressing her and get on with the recital?" Thirty minutes, forty-five minutes. Finally the teacher's wife came out and took off her own golden necklace and put it around my daughter's neck. Caroline was thrilled.

When I let go of my impatience, I realized what a wonderful thing was happening. In Bali children are held in great respect as members of society. Whether a dancer is six or twenty-six, she is equally honored and respected as an artist, one who performs not for the audience but for the gods. The level of respect that Caroline was given as an artist inspired her to dance beautifully. Imagine how you would feel if you were given such respect as a child. Just as the Buddha cultivated patience, respect, and compassion to mature his heart over one hundred thousand lifetimes, we can bring a bit of this to our families and love relationships.

Spiritual practice should not become an excuse to withdraw from life when difficulties arise. Meditation practice of any sort would not get very far if we stopped meditating every time we encountered a difficulty. The capacity for commitment is what carries our practice. In a love relationship such as marriage, commitment is the necessary down payment for success. Commitment does not mean a security pact where love is a business exchange — "I'll be here for you if you don't change too much. if you don't leave me." The commitment in a conscious relationship is to remain together, committed to helping one another grow in love, honoring and fostering the opening of our partner's spirit.

In both child rearing and love relationships, we will inevitably encounter the same hindrances as we do sitting in meditation. We will desire to be somewhere else or with someone else. We will feel aversion, judgment, and fear. We will have periods of laziness and dullness. We will get restless with one another, and we will have doubts. We can name these familiar demons and meet them in the spirit of practice. We can acknowledge the body of fear that underlies them and, together with our partner, speak of these very difficulties as a way to deepen our love.

*Moving into the World*

As our life circumstances change and we learn to find balance in a succession of difficulties, we discover the true meaning of wakefulness and freedom. What better temple can we ask for? We can extend these same principles from family life to the work of our community, to politics, to economics, to global peace work, or to service to the poor. All of these spheres ask us to bring to them the qualities of a Buddha. Can we bring the Buddha into the voting booth where we live; can we act as the Buddha, writing letters to our congressmen and congresswomen; can we share in feeding the hungry; can we walk like the Buddha to demonstrate for peace or justice or care for our environment? The greatest gift we can bring to the challenges of these areas is our wisdom and greatness of heart. Without it, we perpetuate the problems; with it, we can begin to transform the world.

I remember the first anti-Vietnam War demonstration I attended, how the protestors brought the same aggression and hate to the generals and politicians as the generals brought to their battles. We were simply re-creating the war. Yet I believe we can be on the barricades, make strong political statements, place our hearts and bodies in the service of justice, without basing actions on hatred, without creating "us" and "them." Martin Luther King Jr., reminded us never to succumb to the temptations of making people our enemy. "As you press on for justice," he said, "be sure to move with dignity and discipline, using only the weapons of love."

A well-known writer friend was gravely disturbed by the mass destruction of the Persian Gulf War. She wished to respond in as personal and direct a way as possible. So she took her meditation practice out into the square in the center of her town. Every day at noon, in rain, snow, or sun, she would sit peacefully and meditate next to a sign that asked for peace in the Persian Gulf. Some days people shouted at her, some days they joined her, some days she was alone. But no matter, she continued to demonstrate the peace she wanted in her square, day by day.

One Zen master is currently training thousands of ecological and political demonstrators in the principles of sitting and nonviolence. They learn about working with the inevitable conflict and demons that arise, and how to bring the peace and integrity they desire to the process of change. Another spiritual peace worker, in an important meeting with the general who heads the European nuclear forces, began his conversation by saying, "It must be very difficult to bear responsibility for the defense of all the people in Europe." Starting from this initial sense of mutual respect, the dialogue went very well.

We can enter the realm of politics with the integrity of world citizens and the wisdom of a bodhisattva, a being committed to the awakening of all. We can bring our spiritual practice into the streets, into our communities, when we see each realm as a temple, as a place to discover that which is sacred. Suppose you considered your neighborhood to be your temple — how would you treat your temple, and what would be your spiritual task there? Perhaps you would simply pick up litter when you saw it or move rocks out of the road before anyone could strike them. Perhaps you would drive in a mindful sacred way or drive less and use less gas. Perhaps you would greet neighbors with the hospitality that you greet your brothers and sisters within the temple. Perhaps you would organize care for the sick or hungry.

No one says this will be easy. Sitting in meditation is difficult and acting in meditation is equally difficult. It may take years of practice to learn how to enter the family arena or the political arena and stay connected with our deepest compassion. Staying connected takes a particular and conscious effort. Yet, what is sacred and what is true is found here as much as anywhere.

# XI

# Life in the World

by Ramana Maharshi
Edited by David Godman

There is a well-established Hindu tradition that prescribes four stages of life (*āśrama*) for serious spiritual seekers:

1. *Brahmacarya* (celibate study). A long period of scriptural studies prior to marriage, usually in an institution that specializes in Vedic scholarship.

2. *Gṛhastha* (marriage and family). At the conclusion of his studies the aspirant is expected to marry and to discharge his business and household duties conscientiously, but without attachment to them.

3. *Vānaprastha* (forest hermit). When all family obligations have been fulfilled (which usually means when the children are married off), the aspirant may retire to a solitary place, usually a forest, and engage in full-time meditation.

4. *Saṁnyāsa* (wandering monk). In the final stage the seeker drops out of the world completely and becomes a wandering mendicant monk. Having no material, social or financial entanglements the *saṁnyāsī* has theoretically removed all the attachments which previously impeded his progress towards Self-realization.

This time-honored structure sustained the common Indian belief that it was necessary to abandon one's family and take to a meditative life of celibate asceticism if one was seriously interested in realizing the Self. Shri Ramana was asked about this belief many times but he always refused to endorse it. He consistently refused to give his devotees permission to give up their worldly responsibilities in favor of a meditative life and he always insisted that realization was equally accessible to everyone, irrespective of their physical circumstances. Instead of advising physical renunciation he told all his devotees that it would be spiritually more productive for them to discharge their normal duties and obligations with an awareness that there was no individual "I" performing or accepting responsibility for the acts which the body performed. He firmly believed that mental attitude had a greater bearing on spiritual progress than physical circumstances and he persistently discouraged all questioners who felt that a manipulation of their environment, however slight, would be spiritually beneficial.

The only physical changes he ever sanctioned were dietary. He accepted the prevailing Hindu theory of diet which claimed that the type of food consumed affected the quantity and quality of one's thoughts and he recommended a moderate intake of vegetarian food as the most useful aid to spiritual practice.

The Hindu dietary theory which Shri Ramana endorsed classifies different foods according to the mental states that they induce:

1. *Sattva* (purity or harmony): Dairy, produce, fruit, vegetables and cereals are deemed to be *sāttvika* foods. A diet which consists largely of these products helps spiritual aspirants to maintain a still, quiet mind.

2. *Rajas* (activity): *Rajāsika* foods include meat, fish and hot spicy foods such as chilies, onions and garlic. Ingestion of these foods results in an overactive mind.

3. *Tamas* (sluggishness): Foods which are decayed, stale or the product of a fermentation process (e.g. alcohol) are classified as *tāmasika*. Consumption of these foods leads to apathetic, torpid states of mind, which hamper clear decisive thinking.

Q: I have a good mind to resign from service and remain constantly with Shri Bhagavan.

A: Bhagavan is always with you, in you, and you are yourself Bhagavan. To realize this it is neither necessary to resign your job nor run away from home. Renunciation does not imply apparent divesting of costumes, family ties, home, and so on, but renunciation of desires, affection and attachment. There is no need to resign your job, only resign yourself to God, the bearer of the burden of all. One who renounces desires actually merges in the world and expands his love to the whole universe.

Expansion of love and affection would be a far better term for a true devotee of God than renunciation, for one who renounces the immediate ties actually extends the bonds of affection and love to a wider world beyond the borders of caste, creed and race. A *saṁnyāsī* who apparently casts away his clothes and leaves his home does not do so out of aversion to his immediate relations but because of the expansion of his love to others around him. When this expansion comes, one does not feel that one is running away from home, instead one drops from it like a ripe fruit from a tree. Till then it would be folly to leave one's home or job.[1]

Q: How does a householder (*gṛhastha*) fare in the scheme of liberation (*mokṣa*)? Should he not necessarily become a mendicant in order to attain liberation?

A: Why do you think you are a householder? Similar thoughts that you are a wandering monk (*saṁnyāsī*) will haunt you, even if you go out as a *saṁnyāsī*. Whether you continue in the household or renounce it and go to the forest, your mind haunts you. The ego is the source of thought. It creates the body and the world and it makes you think of being the householder. If you renounce, it will only substitute the thought of a monk for that of a householder and the environment of the forest for that of the household. But the mental obstacles are always there for you. They even increase greatly in the new surroundings. It is no help to change the environment. The one obstacle is the mind and it must be overcome whether in the home or in the forest. If you can do it in the forest, why not in the home? Therefore, why change the environment? Your efforts can be made even now, whatever the environment.

Q: Is it possible to enjoy awareness of Reality (*samādhi*) while busy in worldly work?

A: The feeling "I work" is the hindrance. Ask yourself, "Who works?" Remember who you are. Then the work will not bind you; it will go on automatically. Make no effort either to work or to renounce; it is your effort that is the bondage. What is destined to happen will happen. If you are destined not to work, work cannot be had even if you hunt for it. If you are destined to work, you will not be able to avoid it and you will be forced to engage yourself in it. So, leave it to the higher power; you cannot renounce or retain as you choose.

Q: Bhagavan said yesterday that while one is engaged in search of God "within", "outer" work would go on automatically. In the life of Shri Chaitanya it is said that during his lectures to students he was really seeking Krishna within and he forgot all about his body and went on talking of Krishna only. This raises a doubt as to whether work can safely be left to itself. Should one keep part of one's attention on the physical work?

A: The Self is all. Are you apart from the Self? Or can the work go on without the Self? The Self is universal so all actions will go on whether you strain yourself to be engaged in them or not. The work will go on of itself. Thus Krishna told Arjuna that he need not trouble to kill the Kauravas because they were already slain by God. It was not for him to resolve to work and worry himself about it, but to allow his own nature to carry out the will of the higher power.

Q: But the work may suffer if I do not attend to it.

A: Attending to the Self means attending to the work. Because you identify yourself with the body, you think that work is done by you. But the body and its activities, including that work, are not apart from the Self. What does it matter whether you attend to the work or not? When you walk from one place to another you do not attend to the steps you take and yet you find yourself after a time at your goal. You see how the business of walking goes on without your attending to it. So also with other kinds of work.[2]

Q: If one holds the Self in remembrance, will one's actions always be right?

A: They ought to be. However, such a person is not concerned with the right or wrong of actions. His actions are God's and therefore right.

Q: How can my mind be still if I have to use it more than other people do? I want to go into solitude and renounce my headmaster's work.

A: No. You may remain where you are and go on with the work. What is the undercurrent which vivifies the mind, enables it to do all this work? It is the Self. So that is the real source of your activity. Simply be aware of it during your work and do not forget it. Contemplate in the background of your mind even whilst working. To do that, do not hurry, take your own time. Keep the remembrance of your real nature alive, even while working, and avoid haste that causes you to forget. Be deliberate. Practice meditation to still the mind and cause it to become aware of its true relationship to the Self which supports it. Do not imagine it is you who are doing the work. Think that it is the underlying current which is doing it. Identify yourself with the current. If you work unhurriedly, re-collectedly, your work or service need not be a hindrance.[3]

Q: In the early stages would it not be a help to a man to seek solitude and give up his outer duties in life?

A: Renunciation is always in the mind, not in going to forests or solitary places or giving up one's duties. The main thing is to see that the mind does not turn outward but inward. It does not really rest with a man whether he goes to this place or that or whether he gives up his duties or not. All these events happen according to destiny. All the activities that the body is to go through are determined when it first comes into existence. It does not rest with you to accept or reject them. The only freedom you have is to turn your mind inward and renounce activities there.

Q: But is it not possible for something to be a help, especially to a beginner, like a fence round a young tree? For instance, don't our books say that it is helpful to go on pilgrimages to sacred shrines or to get the company of saints (*satsaṅga*)?

A: Who said they are not helpful? Only such things do not rest with you, whereas turning your mind inward does. Many people desire the pilgrimage or *satsaṅga* that you mention, but do they all get it?

Q: Why is it that turning inward alone is left to us and not any outer things?

A: If you want to go to fundamentals, you must inquire who you are and find out who it is who has freedom or destiny. Who are you and why did you get this body that has these limitations?[4]

Q: Is solitude necessary for spiritual practice (*vicāra*)?

A: There is solitude everywhere. The individual is solitary always. His business is to find it out within, not to seek it outside himself.[5]

Solitude is in the mind of man. One might be in the thick of the world and maintain serenity of mind. Such a one is in solitude. Another may stay in a forest, but still be unable to control his mind. Such a man cannot be said to be in solitude. Solitude is a function of the mind. A man attached to desires cannot get solitude wherever he may be, whereas a detached man is always in solitude.

Q: So then, one might be engaged in work and be free from desire and keep up solitude. Is it so?

A: Yes. Work performed with attachment is a shackle, whereas work performed with detachment does not affect the doer. One who works like this is, even while working, in solitude.[6]

Q: Our everyday life is not compatible with such efforts.

A: Why do you think you are active? Take the gross example of your arrival here. You left home in a cart, took a train, alighted at the railway station here, got into a cart there and found yourself in this ashram. When asked, you say that you traveled here all the way from your town. Is it true? Is it not a fact that you remained as you were and there were movements of conveyances all along the way? Just as those movements are confounded with your own, so also are the other activities. They are not your own, they are God's activities.[7]

Q: How can cessation of activity (*nivṛtti*) and peace of mind be attained in the midst of household duties, which are of the nature of constant activity?

A: As the activities of the wise man exist only in the eyes of others and not in his own, although he may be accomplishing immense tasks, he really does nothing. Therefore his activities do not stand in the way of inaction and peace of mind. For he knows the truth that all activities take place in his mere presence and that he does nothing. Hence he will remain as the silent witness of all the activities taking place.[8]

Q: Is it harder for Westerners to withdraw inwards?

A: Yes, they are *rājasika* (mentally overactive) and their energy goes outwards. We must be inwardly quiet, not forgetting the Self, and then externally we can go on with activity. Does a man who is acting on the stage in a female part forget that he is a man? Similarly, we too must play our parts on the stage of life, but we must not identify ourselves with those parts.

Q: How does one remove the spiritual sloth of others?

A: Have you removed your own? Turn your inquiries towards the Self. The force set up within you will operate on others also.[9]

Q: But how can I help another with his problem, his troubles?

A: What is this talk of another — there is only the one. Try to realize that there is no I, no you, no he, only the one Self which is all. If you believe in the problem of another, you are believing in something outside the Self. You will best help him by realizing the oneness of everything rather than by outward activity.[10]

Q: Do you approve of sexual continence?

A: A true celibate (*brahmacārī*) is one who dwells in *Brahman*. Then there is no question of desires any more.

Q: At Shri Aurobindo's ashram there is a rigid rule that married couples are permitted to live there on condition that they have no sexual intercourse.

A: What is the use of that? If it exists in the mind, what use is it to force people to abstain?

Q: Is marriage a bar to spiritual progress?

A: The householder's life is not a bar, but the householder must do his utmost to practice self-control. If a man has a strong desire for the higher life then the sex tendency will subside. When the mind is destroyed, the other desires are destroyed also.[11]

Q: I have committed sexual sin.

A: Even if you have, it does not matter so long as you do not think afterwards that you have done so. The Self is not aware of any sin and renunciation of sex is internal, not merely of the body alone.

Q: I am carried away by the sight of the breasts of a young woman neighbor and I am often tempted to commit adultery with her. What should I do?

A: You are always pure. It is your senses and body which tempt you and which you confuse with your real Self. So first know who is tempted and who is there to tempt. But even if you do commit adultery, do not think about it afterwards, because you are yourself always pure. You are not the sinner.[12]

Q: How do we root out our sex idea?

A: By rooting out the false idea of the body being the Self.

There is no sex in the Self. Be the Self and then you will have no sex troubles.

Q: Can fasting cure sexual desire?

A: Yes, but it is temporary. Mental fast is the real aid. Fasting is not an end in itself. There must be spiritual development side by side. Complete fasting makes the mind too weak. The spiritual quest must be kept up right through a fast if it is to benefit spiritually.[13]

Q: Can one progress spiritually by fasting?

A: Fasting should be chiefly mental (abstention from thoughts). Mere abstinence from food will do no good; it will even upset the mind. Spiritual unfoldment will come rather by regulating eating. But if, during a fast of one month, the spiritual outlook has been maintained, then in about ten days after the breaking of the fast (if it be rightly broken and followed by judicious eating) the mind will become pure and steady, and remain so.[14]

In the early days after my coming here, I had my eyes closed and I was so deeply absorbed in meditation that I hardly knew whether it was day or night. I had no food and no sleep. When there is movement in the body, you need food. If you have food, you need sleep. If there is no movement, you do not need sleep. Very little food is enough to sustain life. That used to be my experience. Somebody or other used to offer me a cup of some liquid diet whenever I opened my eyes. That was all I ever ate. But remember one thing: except when one is absorbed in a state where the mind is motionless, it is not possible to give up sleep or food altogether. When the body and mind are engaged in the ordinary pursuits of life, the body reels if you give up food and sleep.

There are differing theories concerning how much a spiritual student (*sādhaka*) should eat and how much he should sleep. Some say that it is healthy to go to bed at 10 p.m. and wake up at 2 a.m. That means that four hours of sleep is enough. Some say that four hours of sleep is not enough, but that it should be six hours. It amounts to this, that sleep and food should not be taken in excess. If you want to cut off either of them completely, your mind will always be directed towards them. Therefore, the *sādhaka* should do everything in moderation.[15]

There is no harm in eating three to four times a day. But only do not say "I want this kind of food and not that kind" and so on. Moreover, you take these meals in twelve hours of waking whereas you are not eating in twelve hours of sleep. Does sleep lead you to *mukti*? It is wrong to suppose that simple inactivity leads one to *mukti*.[16]

Q: What about diet?

A: Food affects the mind. For the practice of any kind of yoga, vegetarianism is absolutely necessary since it makes the mind more *sāttvika* (pure and harmonious). ...

Q: Generally speaking, what are the rules of conduct that an aspirant should follow?

A: Moderation in food, moderation in sleep, and moderation in speech.[17]

Footnotes:

[1] R. Swarnagiri, *Crumbs from his Table*, p. 43.

[2] T.N. Venkataraman (pub.), *Maharshi's Gospel*, p. 7-8.

[3] P. Brunton, *Conscious Immortality*, p. 130-1.

[4] S. Nagamama, *Letters from Shri Ramanasramama*, p. 211-12.

[5] M. Venkataramiah (comp.), *Talks with Shri Ramana Maharshi*, p. 50.

[6] *Ibid.*, p. 15.

[7] *Ibid.*, p. 80.

[8] S. Natanananda, *Spiritual Instruction of Bhagavan Shri Ramana Maharshi*, p. 17.

[9] P. Brunton, *Conscious Immortality*, p. 123-4.

[10] *Ibid.*, p. 133.

11  *Ibid.*, p. 43. The question about Shri Aurobindo Ashram comes from the original manuscript of the book. It was deleted from the published version.

12  *Ibid.*, p. 133.

13  *Ibid.*, p. 31.

14  'Who', *Maha Yoga*, p. 204.

15  S. Nagamma, *Letters from Shri Ramanasraman*, p. 175-6.

16  P. Brunton, *Conscious Immortality*, p.32.

17  S. Natanananada, *Spiritual Instruction of Bhagavan Shri Ramana Maharshi*, p. 14.

# PART FOUR

# The Golden Years

For the ignorant, old age is winter;
For the learned, old age is the harvest.

*Yiddish saying*

Enjoy the seasons of life.... Each season of life is wonderful if you have learned the lessons of the season before. It is only when you go on with lessons unlearned that you wish for a return.

Peace Pilgrim

There is no finer or more fitting way to spend time during the evening years of life than turning the mind toward reflection and then stilling it in the Silence.

Paul Brunton.

# XII

# Aging and Retirement

by Menachem Mendel Schneerson

*[The following article is taken from the book* Toward a Meaningful Life *which is a practical distillation of the philosophy of Rabbi Menachem Mendel Schneerson, a revered leader and teacher known throughout the world simply as "the Rebbe." Throughout the book, G-d is written with a hyphen instead of an "o", in keeping with the Rebbe's style, based on the belief that even while writing, we must feel a sense of awe, a sense that G-d is above and beyond all our words.]*

*In the spring of 1972, when the Rebbe was about to turn seventy years old, he received many letters from well wishers. Some of them suggested that he consider slowing his very active pace after his many fruitful decades as a leader and activist, that it might be time for him to rest, as do most people his age.*

*The Rebbe, of course, had no such intention. On his seventieth birthday, after a busy day receiving such luminaries as Yitzhak Rabin and HermanWouk (who delivered a personal letter from President Nixon), the Rebbe convened a special gathering. His talk was long, emotional, and intense. True to his style, the Rebbe used a personal issue to deliver a universal message. He emphasized that the elderly must not succumb to conventional wisdom and cease to pursue a productive life. On the contrary, they must use their added years of wisdom and experience to grow "from strength to strength." To shunt the elderly aside is not only cruel, he added, but also foolish, the faster our world*

118

*changes, the more we need the experience and wisdom of our elderly friends and relatives.*

*In 1982, the Rebbe presided over another huge gathering in honor of his birthday, this time his eightieth. He spoke passionately until 3:00 a.m. and still he wasn't through. In a striking testament to the strength of the elderly — and to the idea of exemplifying what one teaches — the Rebbe began distributing study books that had been printed especially for this occasion. There were several thousand men, women, and children present, and the Rebbe patiently handed a book to each one. By the time he finished, the light of dawn was trickling through the windows.*

## Retirement from What?

You have worked very hard for many years. As your physical faculties weaken, shouldn't you be slowing down? Hasn't the time come to reap the rewards of life? Society's solution, of course, is retirement. But have we considered the effects of retirement on our spirits? Why are so many of our elderly so unhappy? Why do they experience such emptiness in their lives? All of us, if we are fortunate, will grow old. Should we look toward that time with enthusiasm or with dread? Before contemplating the later years of your life, you must ask yourself a basic question about life itself. Why am I here? Your attitude toward aging and retirement will depend on how you answer that question.

You may believe that the primary objective of life is to take advantage of its material possibilities and live as comfortably as you can. If so, you might think that you will be content to live out your later years in as much comfort as you can afford. You might see the last years of your life as a time to enjoy the just deserts of a long life of labor.

But why, then, do you often have a nagging feeling of dissatisfaction about spending your days in leisure? Because you were *not* put on earth to live a purely material existence, you were created to refine this material world with truth and virtue, introducing G-dliness into your every moment. This is our life's mission, and it lasts our *entire* life.

If we were to measure life solely in terms of material gain and productivity, then we would inevitably see the physical weakening of old age as a liability. But because man is primarily a spiritual being, whose true wealth is measured in intellectual, emotional, and spiritual gains, we recognize that the *soul* is the primary force in life. And the soul, unlike the body, never ages, it only grows.

As one ages, therefore, he should *not* decrease his level of activity, for spiritually, he is growing ever stronger. Unfortunately, society has taught us to see success in material terms — to think that a millionaire, regardless of his spiritual wealth, is somehow superior to a poor man who is truly wise. We must retrain the way we think, to define success in the more sublime terms of ability and competence, wisdom and experience.

Because man was created to spiritualize the material world, the only way to reach true happiness is through spiritual growth and achievement. And that means giving to others, loving and sharing, finding a deeper meaning in everything you do, and recognizing G-d in all your ways.

Recognize the prominence of your timeless soul. This is the key to understanding the aging process, the key with which we open the door of opportunity in our twilight years. Human productivity is a direct result of human creativity, and human creativity is a direct result of the spiritual energies of the soul. "Every person was created to toil," as the sages say. However, this toil takes on different forms in our life cycles. As one ages and his physical strength wanes, his toil and productivity need to be expressed through spiritual achievements. So if a human being reaches a certain age, whether it is fifty-five or sixty-five or seventy-five, and suddenly announces, "I'm going to retire," the question must be asked. Retire from what? Ambition? Creativity — From your soul? Such an attitude means that you are simply preparing to die, which is unacceptable for a person who comes into this world with a mission to produce. One does not retire from life.

The argument for retirement is an erroneous one. It assumes that our goal in life is to amass the right amount of wealth so that we can shut down our productivity at a certain age and revel in our material success and free time. This is not to say that we should not enjoy the fruits of our labor — only that we should never forget the reason that the labor has been done in the first place. Nor must we devote our entire lives to earning a living. But we should never abandon the world of work and productivity for a world of inactivity, a world that doesn't challenge us, a world that isolates us from our spiritual quest.

## How Attitudes are Formed

Each phase of life, of course, has a unique set of characteristics and needs. That is why we must take great care in educating a child, for his mind is so impressionable; that is why we must properly channel the fiery spirit of young people, for it is so strong; that is why we develop careers and raise families during middle age, because we have by then achieved the necessary blend of maturity and ability.

So too does the twilight of our lives have its inherent strengths. Sometimes, of course, modern society makes us forget this. Think about how we constantly celebrate the image of youth, how it has come to stand for everything that is energetic and desirable. This has an obvious demoralizing effect on the elderly and, by extension, on society in general. If we value the physical vitality of youth more than intelligence and wisdom, more than the *spiritual* vitality of an experienced soul, what does that tell us about *all* our standards?

So there are two vastly divergent views on aging — that is, "You are old and worn out, thus useless" versus "You are wise and experienced, thus indispensable." The Bible assures us that old age is a virtue and a blessing. We are told to respect all the elderly, regardless of their scholarship and piety,[1] because each year of life yields wisdom and experience that the most accomplished young person cannot possibly yet possess.

But in many societies today old age has come to be a liability. Youth, meanwhile, is considered the highest credential in every field from business to government, where a younger generation insists on learning from its own mistakes instead of standing on the shoulders of their elders. At fifty, a person is considered "over the hill," and is already enduring insinuations that his job might be better filled by someone twenty-five years younger. Society, in effect, is dictating that one's later years be marked by inactivity and decline. The aged are encouraged to move to retirement villages and nursing homes; after decades of achievement, they are thought to be of little use, their knowledge and talent suddenly deemed worthless.

On the surface, this modern attitude may seem at least partially justified. Is it not a fact that a person physically weakens as he or she advances in years? Is it not an inescapable fact that the physical body of a seventy-year-old is not the physical body of a thirty-year-old?

But is a person's worth to be measured by his physical prowess? This question goes beyond the issue of how we *treat* the elderly, our attitude toward them reflects our very concept of value. If a person's physical strength has waned while his wisdom and insight have grown, do we consider this an improvement or a decline?

Certainly, if a person's priorities in life are material, then the body's physical weakening means a deterioration of spirit as well — a descent into boredom, futility, and despair. But when one regards the body as an accessory to the soul, the very opposite is true. The spiritual growth of old age invigorates the body. And the later years allow us to positively reorder our priorities, which is difficult to do during middle age, when the quest for material gains is at its peak.

The idea of retirement is rooted in society's notion that life is composed of productive and nonproductive periods. The first twenty to thirty years of life are seen as a time when a person is training for a productive life. The next thirty to forty years are when his creative energies are realized, he begins to return what has been invested in him by his now passive elders, and, in turn, begins investing in the still passive younger generation. Finally, as he enters his later years, he puts his period of "real" achievement behind him. If a creative urge still strikes, he is advised to find some harmless hobby to fill his time. Indeed, time has become something to be *filled*. In a sense, he has come full circle to childhood — once again, he is a passive recipient in a world shaped by the initiative of others.

The time to passively enjoy the fruits of one's labor does indeed have its time and place — in the world to come. The very fact that G-d has granted a person a single additional day of bodily life means that he or she has not yet concluded his or her mission in life, that there is still much to achieve in this world.

A hardworking adult may nostalgically remember childhood as a time of freedom from responsibility and toil. As we grow, however, we disdain such "freedom," wanting to do something real and creative. Similarly, the promise of a "happy retirement" is a cruel myth, for we know true happiness only when we are creatively contributing to our world. The weakened physical state of old age, therefore, is not a sentence of inactivity, but a challenge to find new — and superior — means of achievement.

> An aged man who could barely walk asked a group of young men to help carry his packages. Instead, they began to mock him "Old people like you need to stay home," one of them said, "You are useless and just a burden to the rest of us." The young men were musicians, and a few days later, they went off into the woods to find a quiet place to play. As they were walking they heard from a far-off clearing a rich, beautiful voice singing a haunting melody. From a distance, they finally saw the singer, sitting alone on a rock, singing into the

heavens. As they drew closer, they saw that it was none other than the old man.

## The Steps to Take

We must always remember that, spiritually, we are all united. The soul of a seventy-year-old shares the same spiritual space as that of a seven-year-old or a twenty-seven-year-old. And so, just as the seven-year-old must learn to respect his elders, and just as the twenty-seven-year-old must learn that his decisions greatly affect the elderly, the elderly themselves must recognize their role. That role is not a passive one, in fact, the later years of life are filled with opportunities that may have totally escaped our sight until we are upon them.

Just because we stop going to work every day does not mean that we stop using our body and soul to fulfill our G-dly mission. The same energy that you once spent worrying about your competition or planning your business can now be devoted to projects that you never had time for, projects that shine a light of goodness on those around you. Remember, the experience of an older man or woman — whether in business, in civic matters, or in the home — is priceless.

Even before society begins to appreciate the value of age, the elderly must take their lives into their own hands. The elderly must learn to exercise their own convictions as strongly as modern society exerts its own considerable force. Do not, therefore, feel defeated by your age and its physical effects. Do not heed those who say that you are less useful because you are less physically strong than you once were. Do not listen to those who claim that nothing more is expected of you than leisurely walks and playing golf, than spending your days and years doing nothing.

Our twilight years are just what the name implies — the beautiful culmination of a day well spent. In childhood, we peek into an uncertain future, eager to learn but inexperienced and dependent on others. In the twilight years, we look back at what we have learned, confident and eager to impart this wisdom unto others. Just as you may need a younger person's helping hand in your physical life, that person needs *your* helping hand in his spiritual life.

Yet retirement, mandatory or otherwise, is a fact of modern life. Year after year, it condemns valuable human resources — indeed, our *most* valuable human resources — to a state of stagnation. What is one to do in the face of such human and social tragedy? Should one embark on a campaign to change this practice and the value system behind it, or should one look for the brighter side of retirement?

Indeed, we must do both. We must change the attitudes of society's leaders, but we must also change the elderly's perception of themselves. We must tell them. Not only are you not useless, but you are a greater asset to society than ever before. At the same time, we must exploit the opportunities of retirement. For those men and women seeking to fill their time constructively, let us establish study centers in every community, and let us set up classes and workshops in every nursing home and retirement village. Education, like productivity, is a lifelong endeavor. Such an intensive pursuit of prayer and study will illuminate the elderly's self-worth and potential, transforming them from cast-asides into beacons of light for their families and communities. Indeed, if properly utilized, retirement can become one of the most productive periods in a long life.

*Rejuvenate the Spirit*

We must remember that no matter how weak our bodies may become, the soul remains strong, constantly yearning for nourishment. You should nourish your soul by setting aside a special time each day to study and pray, to feed your mind and heart. You should also designate time to share your experiences with younger people, and encourage others to do the same. If you are sincere in your effort to communicate, a younger person will recognize the validity of what you have to say, and make a genuine effort to respond. Spend time with your grandchildren and share your life with them. Gently educate them in the priorities of life that only you can impart. Simply love and enjoy them, and allow them to love and enjoy you.

Look upon these activities not merely as a way to fill your spare time, but as a means to feed your soul, to rejuvenate your spirit. More and more, medicine is teaching us that our physical health is dependent on our spiritual health. So do not succumb to your body's voice, or to the discouraging voices of those around you. Remember that age is dignity, that age is wisdom. Physical strength may be ephemeral, but good deeds are eternal. And every good deed ultimately affects the entire world.

It is time to take a new look at the elderly. To take a new look at retirement. To take a new look at the very essence of life. Of all people, it is perhaps the elderly who most need — and who can best teach us all — to lead a meaningful life.

*In the summer of 1980, when the Rebbe was seventy-eight, he called for the establishment of study centers for the aged. Hundreds of such centers — named, at the Rebbe's suggestion, Tiferet Zkeinim ("Glory of the Aged") — have since been founded in every corner of the globe. Here, the elderly revel in each other's wisdom and face new intellectual challenges daily.*

Footnote:

[1]    Leviticus 19:32. Talmud, Kidushin 32b.

# XIII

# Each is Great
# in His Own Place

### by Swami Vivekananda

A certain king used to inquire of all the *saṁnyāsin* that came to his country, "Which is the greater man — he who gives up the world and becomes a *saṁnyāsin*, or he who lives in the world and performs his duties as a householder?" Many wise men sought to solve the problem. Some asserted that the *saṁnyāsin* was the greater, upon which the king demanded that they should prove their assertion. When they could not, he ordered them to marry and become householders. Then others came and said, "The householder who performs his duties is the greater man." Of them, too, the king demanded proof. When they could not give them, he made them also settle down as householders.

At last there came a young *saṁnyāsin*, and the king inquired of him also. He answered, "Each, O King, is equally great in his own place."

"Prove this to me," demanded the king.

"I will prove it to you," said the *saṁnyāsin*, "but you must first come and live as I do for a few days, that I may be able to prove to you what I say."

The king consented and followed the *saṁnyāsin* out of his own territory. They passed through many other countries until they came to a great kingdom. In the capital of that kingdom a great ceremony was going on. The king and the *saṁnyāsin* heard the noise of drums and music, and also heard the criers. The

127

people were assembled in the streets in gala dress, and a great proclamation was being made. The king and the *saṁnyāsin* stood there to see what was going on. The crier was proclaiming loudly that the princess, daughter of the king of that country, was about to choose a husband from among those assembled before her.

It was an old custom in India for princesses to choose husbands in this way. Each princess had certain ideas of the sort of man she wanted for a husband. Some would have the handsomest man, others would have only the most learned, others again the richest, and so on. All the princes of the neighborhood would put on their best attire and present themselves before her. Sometimes they too had their own criers to enumerate their virtues and the reasons why they hoped the princess would choose them. The princess would be taken around on a throne, in the most splendid array, and would look at them and hear about them. If she was not pleased with what she saw and heard, she would say to her bearers, "Move on," and would take no more notice of the rejected suitor. If, however, the princess was pleased with any one of them, she would throw a garland of flowers over him and he would become her husband.

The princess of the country to which our king and the *saṁnyāsin* had come was having one of these interesting ceremonies. She was the most beautiful princess in the world, and her husband would be ruler of the kingdom after her father's death. The idea of this princess was to marry the handsomest man, but she could not find the right one to please her. Several times these meetings had taken place, but the princess could not select a husband. This meeting was the most splendid of all. More people than ever before had attended it. The princess came in on a throne, and the bearers carried her from place to place. She did not seem to care for anyone, and everyone became disappointed that this meeting also was going to be a failure.

Just then a young man, a *saṁnyāsin*, handsome as if the sun had come down to the earth, came and stood in one corner of the assembly, watching what was going on. The throne with the princess came near him, and as soon as she saw the handsome *saṁnyāsin*, she stopped and threw the garland over him. The young *saṁnyāsin* seized the garland and threw it off, exclaiming: "What nonsense is this? I am a *saṁnyāsin*. What is marriage to me?" The king of that country thought that perhaps this man was poor and so dared not marry the princess, and said to him, "With my daughter goes half my kingdom now, and the whole kingdom after my death!" and put the garland on the *saṁnyāsin* again. The young man threw it off once more, saying, "Nonsense! I do not want to marry," and walked quickly away from the assembly.

Now the princess had fallen so much in love with this young man that she said, "I must marry this man or I shall die," and she went after him to bring him back. Then our other *saṁnyāsin*, who had brought the king there, said to him, "King, let us follow this pair." So they walked after them, but at a good distance behind. The young *saṁnyāsin* who had refused to marry the princess walked out into the country for several miles. When he came to a forest and entered into it, the princess followed him, and the other two followed them. Now this young *saṁnyāsin* was well acquainted with that forest and knew all the intricate paths in it. He suddenly passed into one of these and disappeared, and the princess could not discover him. After trying to find him for a long time, she sat down under a tree and began to weep, for she did not know the way out. Then our king and the other *saṁnyāsin* came up to her and said: "Do not weep. We will show you the way out of this forest, but it is too dark for us to find it now. Here is a big tree. Let us rest under it, and in the morning we will go early and show you the road."

*Sacrificing for Others*

Now a little bird and his wife and their three young ones lived on that tree in a nest. This little bird looked down and saw the three people under the tree and said to his wife: "My dear, what shall we do? Here are some guests in the house, and it is winter, and we have no fire." So he flew away and got a bit of burning firewood in his beak and dropped it before the guests, to which they added fuel and made a blazing fire. But the little bird was not satisfied. He said again to his wife: "My dear, what shall we do? There is nothing to give these people to eat, and they are hungry. We are householders; it is our duty to feed anyone who comes to the house. I must do what I can. I will give them my body." So he plunged into the midst of the fire and perished. The guests saw him falling and tried to save him, but he was too quick for them.

The little bird's wife saw what her husband did, and she said: "Here are three persons and only one little bird for them to eat. It is not enough. It is my duty as a wife not to let my husband's effort go in vain. Let them have my body also." Then she fell into the fire and was burned to death.

Then the three baby birds, when they saw what was done and that there was still not enough food for the three guests, said: "Our parents have done what they could and still it is not enough. It is our duty to carry on the work of our parents. Let our bodies go too." And they all dashed down into the fire also.

Amazed at what they saw, the three people could not of course eat these birds. They passed the night without food, and in the morning the king and the *saṁnyāsin* showed the princess the way out of the forest, and she went back to her father.

Then the *saṁnyāsin* said to the king: "King, you have seen that each is great in his own place. If you want to live in the world, live like those birds, ready at any moment to sacrifice yourself for others. If you want to renounce the world, be like that young man to whom the most beautiful woman and a kingdom were nothing. If you want to be a householder, hold your life as sacrifice for the welfare of others, and if you choose the life of renunciation, do not even look at beauty and money and power. Each is great in his own place, but the duty of the one is not the duty of the other. (*Complete Works of Swami Vivekananda* I: 47-51)

# XIV

# Saṁnyāsa: Inner and Outer

## by Swami Tyagananda

*Saṁnyāsa* means renunciation of everything. When you renounce everything — all worldly relationships, possessions, attachments and supports — you stand alone. You find the same
idea when you trace the origin of the word monasticism. It is
derived from the Greek *monos*, meaning alone, solitary. A lot of
other words associated with monasticism also come from the
same root, *monos*.[1] They all indicate the idea of solitude and iso-
lation. This solitude need not necessarily imply absolute isola-
tion such as that of a hermit in the desert or in the forest-cave. It
is basically an inner solitude in which one is separated from all
worldly values. Whoever realizes this inner solitude, whoever
intensely experiences in his heart this sense of being alone, is a
monastic.

It is not so easy to know and feel that you are alone. There
are any number of factors that prevent you from feeling your
aloneness. You have your blood relations: father, mother, brothers, and sisters. Then there are the other relationships you subse-
quently forge: as a husband or a wife with children and grandchildren. And you have your friends and colleagues, superiors
and subordinates, teachers and students, and even enemies. You
feel yourself connected to them in one way or the other. You also
feel identified with your domestic pets, your property, your new
car, your favorite singer, your garden, your country. Then you
have your likes, your dislikes, your preferences — one can go on

and on. All these things are a part of your life you simply cannot wish away. Even if you separate yourself from others physically, you cannot be alone. The real problem is in the mind. And the simple fact is that your mind is afraid to be alone. So even if you are living alone and are in need of company, all you have to do is to switch on your TV set and peep through this "window to the world," and drive away the neurotic feeling of loneliness that may occasionally creep through your veins.

To realize your aloneness, all the factors that prevent you from doing so must be negated. How is this negation brought about? This question is difficult to answer, or there is no one way in which this takes place. Somehow — how exactly one cannot say, but somehow — some people realize all the so-called relationships in this world are superficial and all identification of any sort with any living or non-living thing is plain delusion. Sometimes this realization comes spontaneously, even from an early age, due to the power of thought impressions (*saṁskāra*) from a previous life. In a few cases it may come suddenly and overnight the person's life gets a new orientation. The story of Lalababu is well-known in Bengal. A rich man, he was suddenly "awakened" from a stray remark he heard on the roadside, and realized that in spite of all his wealth and achievements, his life was one big zero. All the values he held dear until then vanished, he realized the "inner solitude," gave up his belongings, settled down in Vrindaban and died a great saint. But such cases of sudden conversion are rare. The majority has to learn the hard way. In most cases it requires persistent blows from the world to awaken man to the reality of his being alone. *Māyā*, the inscrutable, cosmic delusive power, manipulates things in such a way that every time you feel yourself alone you are made to forget it somehow and you carry on blissfully for a while until the next blow comes.

The realization of being alone may also come as a result of discrimination and deep thinking. Everyone has the capacity to think but not everyone utilizes fully this wonderful power. Even those that do think, usually exercise the thinking faculty only on matters related to the objective universe. Very few turn this light of thinking inward and focus it on their own selves and ask fundamental questions. Richard Bach, the famous author of *Jonathan Livingston Seagull*, gives a very practical suggestion in one of his lesser-known books. He says:

> The simplest questions are the most profound. Where were you born? Where is your home? Where are you going? What are you doing? Think about these once in a while, and watch your answers change.[2]

When these questions begin to rattle in your brain, the effect can be quite unsettling. Everything begins to slip through your fingers. All relationships, all possessions suddenly become hollow and meaningless. Through stories and parables great saints have always taught the superficiality and frailty of all worldly relationships. And if all this gives too gloomy a picture to you, just think how far and how long can all your relations, friends and well-wishers accompany you. When death calls on you, it is going to take you alone. No, not even one of your closest buddies can or would like to accompany you beyond the portals of death. At the most they may accompany your corpse up to the cremation-ground or the graveyard and weep for a few days. The journey beyond is your own, to be done all alone. What will accompany you on this journey is your character, the power generated through righteous living. Manu, the ancient law-giver says:

> Righteousness is the only friend that accompanies you after death. Everything else perishes with the death of the body. (*Manu Smṛti*, VIII:17.)

Whether the realization of being alone comes to you spontaneously or through some cataclysmic life-transforming incident, whether it comes to you gradually after getting repeated rebuffs from the world or as a result of discriminative thinking, the effect is the same. It cuts you off from the conventional stream of life in which millions and millions of people seem to be sailing smoothly but unconsciously. Getting a glimpse of the "inner solitude" is the first effort of the soul to become conscious and to awake to the higher levels of reality.

It is certainly a difficult period, because you are coming out of the conventional, unconscious stream of life, but have not yet entered the spiritual, conscious stream. For a while the neophyte appears to be just stranded. He is assailed with doubts, inner conflicts, and bouts of forgetfulness. This is because usually the realization of being alone is only partial. Former attachments and habits try to drag you back into the unconscious stream of the world. A tug-of-war ensues and much depends on your inner strength, patience, and perseverance. If you are overpowered, back you go and fall into the stream of worldly life. Perhaps you make another attempt to get out. Or perhaps you give up hope, surrender the memory of your aloneness, and float along merrily in the unconscious stream of life. But if you are a hero and are determined to fight to the finish, you won't give up. There is nothing that a strong will cannot conquer. If you have the will to succeed, succeed you must. All hurdles gradually melt away and your aloneness leads you to the next step: renunciation.

*Renunciation*

Renunciation is the real beginning of religion. Listen to the words of Swami Vivekananda:

> ... tremendous purity, that tremendous renunciation is the one secret of spirituality. "Neither through wealth, nor through progeny, but through renunciation alone is immortality to be reached," say the Vedas. "Sell all that thou hast and give to the poor, and follow me," says Christ. So all great saints and prophets have expressed it, and have carried it out in their lives. How can great spirituality come without that renunciation? Renunciation is the background of all religious thought wherever it be, and you will always find that as this idea of

renunciation lessens, the more will the senses creep into the field of religion, and spirituality will decrease in the same ratio.[3]

What does renunciation mean? If you understand by it merely "giving up," renunciation would become only a negative virtue. Doesn't it have a positive content as well? Yes, it has. Renunciation does not mean just "giving up," it means "giving up the lower for the sake of the higher." You give up the unreal for the sake of the Real. You give up the impermanent for the sake of the Eternal. In short, you give up the world for the sake of God. After describing what true renunciation means, Shri Ramakrishna asked a devotee in order to test him: "Tell me, what is the meaning of renunciation?" He was pleased when the devotee replied:

Renunciation does not mean simply dispassion for the world. It means dispassion for the world and *also* longing for God.[4]

Moreover, true dispassion for the world cannot come without a genuine longing for God. The two are inseparably interconnected. Here is the testimony of St. Simeon (10th century AD) whose copious writings are included in the Russian version of the *Philokalia*:

Whoever wants to hate the world must love God with the innermost depths of his soul, and acquire a constant memory of Him, for nothing can more strongly urge a man to renounce everything gladly and turn away from worldly things as from dung.[5]

True renunciation is, therefore, always a spontaneous phenomenon. It cannot be achieved by labored efforts. You don't really renounce things yourself; things drop away from you on their own. When and how does this happen? To know this you must remember that you are attached to only that which holds some meaning for you. When things lose their meaning and value, when they become irrelevant and useless to you, you automatically become detached from them. As long as you relish and thrive on worldly puppets and sensual supports, you cannot detach yourself from them. The beginning of the realization of your aloneness provides the first spark to ignite the spirit of detachment in you. You intuitively realize that there is a life higher than the type you have been leading so far. When the awareness of the possibility of higher life dawns on you, detachment becomes easier, almost spontaneous. In fact, the two — realization of your aloneness and detachment from the world — then onwards proceed simultaneously, each strengthening the other. The more you feel the inner solitude, the more detached you become, and the more detached you become, the more you feel the inner solitude. And as a result of this mutual reinforcement, the awareness of the higher life becomes stronger and stronger.

> It is always for greater joy that you give up the lesser [says Vivekananda]. This is practical religion — the attainment of freedom, renunciation. ... Renounce the lower so that you may get the higher. ... Renounce! Renounce! Sacrifice! Give up! Not for zero. Nor for nothing. But to get the higher. But who can do this? You cannot, until you have got the higher. You may talk. You may struggle. You may try to do things. But renunciation comes by itself when you have got the higher. Then the lesser falls away by itself. This is practical religion. What else? Cleaning streets and building hospitals? Their value consists only in this renunciation. And there is no end to renunciation. The difficulty is they try to put a limit to it — thus far and no farther. But there is no limit to this renunciation.[6]

Here Swamiji is obviously emphasizing that unless you give up *all* of the unreal, the Supreme Reality cannot be revealed to you. In spiritual life halfway measures don't work. You've got to make up your mind and choose between God and the world. You can't have your cake and eat it. Renunciation to be effective and fruitful, cannot be fenced and limited. If you want God to come in, mammon has to go out, fully and irrevocably. He shouldn't be allowed to stand even on the threshold.

> Where God is there is no other [Swamiji continues]. Where the world is there is no God. These two will never unite. Like light and darkness. That is what I have understood from Christianity and the life of the Teacher [Jesus Christ]. Is that not Buddhism? Is that not Hinduism? Is that not Mohammedanism? Is that not the teaching of all the great sages and teachers?[7]

Renunciation is basically an internal process. Inwardly a revolution takes place in your attitudes and responses, but outwardly no one may even notice it. You continue with your duties and obligations as before, but your approach to life has changed. In a few cases, this internal renunciation (*antar-samnyāsa*) is followed by external renunciation as well. Thus we have two types of renunciation: inner renunciation and inner + outer renunciation. It is the second type that society conventionally accepts as belonging to monasticism. Those with only inner renunciation may not be regarded as monks and nuns by society, but that does not make any difference to the strength and validity of their spiritual realization. Here are Shri Ramakrishna's words of assurance:

> You may ask, "Is there any difference between the realizations of two *jñānīs*, one a householder and the other a monk?" The reply is that the two belong to one class. Both of them are *jñānīs* they have the same experience.[8]

It is clear that what matters is inner renunciation. That is what Shri Ramakrishna always emphasized:

> Mental renunciation is the essential thing. That, too, makes one a *samnyāsī*. ... But one must set fire to one's desires. Then alone can one succeed.[9]

Those who renounce only internally are "hidden yogis," said Shri Ramakrishna, and those with both inner and outer renunciation are "revealed yogis." The householder, he said, may be a "hidden yogi." None recognizes him. He renounces only men-

*137*

tally, not outwardly. How should he live in the world? Shri Ramakrishna advises to all those who cannot take to formal monasticism for one reason or other:

> Do all your duties, but keep your mind on God. Live with all — with wife and children, father and mother — and serve them. Treat them as if they were very dear to you, but know in your heart of hearts that they do not belong to you. A maidservant in the house of a rich man performs all the household duties, but her thoughts are fixed on her own home in her native village. She brings up her master's children as if they were her own. She even speaks of them as "my Rama" or "my Hari." But in her own mind she knows very well that they do not belong to her at all.
>
> The tortoise moves about in the water. But can you guess where her thoughts are? They are on the bank, where her eggs are lying. Do all your duties in the world, but keep your mind on God.
>
> First rub your hands with oil and then break open the jackfruit; otherwise they will be smeared with its sticky milk. First secure the oil of divine love, and then set your hands to the duties of the world.
>
> Together with this, you must practice discrimination. Objects of lust and greed are impermanent. God is the only Eternal Substance. What does a man get with money? Food, clothes, and a dwelling-place — nothing more. You cannot realize God with its help. Therefore money can never be the goal of life. That is the process of discrimination.[10]

If one succeeds in translating into practice the above teachings of Shri Ramakrishna, perfection in inner renunciation (*antar-saṁnyāsa*) is assured. As for taking up formal vows of *saṁnyāsa*, Shri Ramakrishna advised that there was no point in forcing oneself into it.[11] This lends credence to what we said earlier: renunciation must come naturally and spontaneously.

The popular belief is that only those with greater renunciation take to formal monasticism, while others hesitate to plunge into it. There may be some truth in this, but to accept this belief unreservedly would be wrong, for there have been many exceptions to this. What seems more reasonable — and this is the view held by Shri Ramakrishna — is that whether one renounces only mentally or takes up formal monastic vows depends on the will of God.[12]

Here a note of warning must be sounded. There are two dangers one must guard against. First, mistaking your own will — more correctly, your *lack* of will — as the "will of God." Only one who sees— *sees*, not just talks of the "will of God" behind everything happening to him and around him can really speak about it. Others use it merely as a shield to defend themselves or as a cloak to hide their own weaknesses. This is plain deceit, unconscious though it may be in a few cases. The second danger is to deceive your own self and others by claiming that you already possess mental renunciation when in fact you don't. There is no instrument to measure your mental renunciation and if you are good at posing you can easily fool the gullible. Believe it or not, many are so good at posing and so gullible at the same time that they manage to fool themselves as well. But then deceit has no place in spiritual life. Truth remains far, far away from such people.

How do you protect yourself from falling prey to these dangers? By being honest. It is not enough to be honest while dealing with others. You've got to be honest while dealing with your own self too. You must have the courage to face your own weaknesses, failures, and lapses. Accept yourself as you are. Self-acceptance is the first step in spiritual life. One reason why people dread the inner solitude is that they are afraid to face themselves. When you feel alone there is no one but your own self to be encountered. And in the absence of self-acceptance, encountering your self can be a most frightening or depressing experience. People usually avoid this catastrophic situation through various escape-routes such as seeking external company or turning to novels and light literature or to some other forms of entertainment. The idea is to keep oneself always busy with something or the other. Much of the craze for even social service is not so much due to genuine love and concern for the poor and the suffering as due to the frantic fear of being left alone to face one's self in the inner solitude of one's heart. Your self can be either your friend or your enemy, says Lord Krishna in the *Bhagavad Gītā*, VI:5. It is you who decide what the relation ought to be. To have someone as your friend you must make him feel he's accepted, and he must feel that you understand him, love him, care for him and are interested in him. See whether this is true between you and your self. The main point is to get rid of self-alienation, which is the prime hurdle in spiritual life. Once your self becomes your friend, it protects you from the two dangers mentioned earlier. …

*Wandering Inward*

Let us go back to what we said about renunciation. What do we exactly mean by detachment from all worldly values, relationships and associations? When does such detachment become perfect? To answer this, you ask yourself another question: *What* is it that connects me to the world? The answer comes: only two things — my body and my mind. When the fire of renunciation begins to rage within you, it may apparently seem that you are detaching yourself from persons and things belonging to the world outside. But the truth is that the real detachment is occurring somewhere nearer than is immediately obvious. Your detachment from the world is directly proportional to your detachment from your body and mind. It is your identification with your body and mind that is the source of all attachment. It is only when this identification goes away, or is at least considerably weakened, that renunciation becomes natural, spontaneous.

Vedanta says that the *real* you is different from your body and your mind. To know that you are different from your body is not too difficult. After all, none of us is dumb enough to imagine that the body is going to last eternally. You may not like to think about it: that is another matter. But you know for certain that whether your body lays in a coffin several feet underground or is reduced to a heap of ashes at the cremation-ground, *you* are going to live on. So at least intellectually you know you are different from your body. What is more difficult is to know that you are also different from your mind. Mere reasoning in this case is not sufficient because the faculty of reason is itself a part of your mind. Obviously, perfect awareness of your being someone different from both body and mind is not the result of an intellectual exercise, but of a super-sensuous experience.

Our teachers say that this is the first spiritual experience the renunciate gets — the experience of his true inner Self (*pratyagātman*), which is effulgent, pure, and completely different from body and mind. This experience comes as a result of a disciplined life of purity (*brahmacarya*), burning spiritual aspiration (*vyākulatā*), and intense prayer (*prārthanā*). It is only now, when you have got hold of the *real* you — your true Self (*jivātman*) — that you go forth in search of the Supreme Self (*Paramātman*).

This is a special kind of "going forth." It is called *pravrajana*, literally meaning wandering. It is often wrongly associated with the life of wandering mendicants, who travel from place to place and subsist on alms. *Pravrajana* is wandering all right, but it is basically a wandering *inward*, when the awakened inner Self goes in search of the Supreme Self. This is the purpose of monastic life. It is a search, a diligent search for higher consciousness that culminates in discovering the "eternal relation" that exists between the reality in you and the reality behind all creation. *Advaita Vedānta* maintains that in the course of your inner wandering you may discover different stages or levels of relationship, but your wandering stops — or rather, it reaches a point where there is no beyond when you discover that the relation is really one of identity. Only then does the significance of the great Vedantic truths (*mahāvākya*) become clear.[13] It is one thing to understand these truths intellectually and quite another to intuit them in the depths of one's being. The latter becomes possible only when *pravrajana* reaches its fulfillment.

Once your roots are discovered, once you have realized the eternal relation between the soul and eternal God, the scene begins to shift. You are now ready to embrace what you had renounced earlier. All the apparent contradictions stand resolved. In that state, says Vivekananda, all difficulties vanish. All the perplexities of the heart are smoothed away. All delusion disappears. *Māyā*, instead of being a horrible, hopeless dream, becomes beautiful, and this earth, instead of being a prison-house, becomes our playground. Dangers and difficulties, even all sufferings, become deified and show us their real nature. They show us that behind everything, as the substance of everything, He is standing, and that He is the one real Self.[14]

Your realization of being alone reaches logical fulfillment. The "flight of the alone to the alone" is over when the ALONE alone remains. You are alone but not lonely, because you are not separated from anyone or anything. You are alone, only because there is no "other." And whatever "other" there appears to be, is none but you yourself. What a grand state that must be! Even to think of it gives so much joy! How infinitely more blissful it will be when you actually realize it in the depths of your being! No, you don't renounce anything anymore, for you are all and everything. There is nothing besides you which could be renounced. You began the spiritual quest by renouncing, by negating, by separating. You now end it by embracing, by affirming, by unifying. Never short of illustrations, Shri Ramakrishna describes this situation in a way that only he could:

> First of all you must discriminate, following the method of *neti*, *neti*: "He is not the five elements, nor the sense-organs, nor the mind, nor the intelligence, nor the ego. He is beyond all these cosmic principles." You want to climb to the roof; then you must eliminate and leave behind all the steps, one by one. The steps are by no means the roof. But after reaching

the roof you find that the steps are made of the same materials — brick, lime, and brick-dust — as the roof. It is the Supreme *Brahman* that has become the universe and its living beings and the twenty-four cosmic principles. That which is *Ātman* has become the five elements.[15]

The realization of absolute freedom (*mukti*) is the one goal of monastic life. Freedom, freedom, freedom — is the cry of every soul. While the world, blindfolded by the veil of petty desires and passions, unconsciously searches for freedom in wrong places and in wrong ways, a monastic does it consciously in a right place and in a right way, guided as he is by his Guru, scriptures, and his own awakened power of spiritual intuition.

Footnotes:

[1]  Monk (*monachos*), nun (*monache*), monasticism (*monachikon*), monastery (*monasterion*).

[2]  Richard Bach, *Illusion: The Adventures of a Reluctant Messiah*. p. 47.

[3]  *Complete Works of Swami Vivekananda*, IV:183-84.

[4]  *Gospel of Shri Ramakrishna*, tr. Swami Nikhilananda, p. 506.

[5]  Writings from *The Philokalia on Prayer of the Heart*, tr. E. Kadloubovsky and E. H. Palmer. p. 99.

[6]  *Complete Works of Swami Vivekananda*, IV:244.

[7]  *Ibid.*

[8]  *Gospel of Shri Ramakrishna*, p. 857.

[9]  *Ibid.*, p. 938.

[10]  *Ibid.*, p. 81-82.

[11]  See *ibid.* p. 549.

[12]  See *ibid.*, p. 649.

[13]  The four *mahāvākya* are: Thou art That (*tat tvam asi*), I am *Brahman* (*aham Brahmāsmi*), *Brahman* is Consciousness (*prajñānām Brahma*), This Self is *Brahman* (*ayam ātma Brahman*).

[14]  See *Complete Works of Swami Vivekananda*, II:129.

[15]  *Gospel of Shri Ramakrishna*, p. 417-18.

# XV

# The Glory of Saṁnyāsa

## by Swami Tapovanam

In Buddhism as well as in Hinduism, *saṁnyāsa* and solitary life were treated at one time as most worthy of reverence. Some historians maintain, with sound reason, that *saṁnyāsa* gained such firm hold on Hinduism, which was previously devoted to a life of Vedic rites, sacrifices and action, as a result of imitating Buddhist practices and ideas. Even as many educated moderns criticize the renunciation of action, various schools of thought in the distant past also had found fault with *saṁnyāsa* as unscientific and improper.

For example, there were the integrationists (*Sāmucya Vādīs*) who argued vehemently that, even conceding knowledge of *Brahman* to be the means of liberation, such knowledge should go hand in hand with action towards the goal, and that there is nothing essentially irreconcilable between them. The people of this way of thinking were totally opposed to the renunciation of action, but the advocates of *saṁnyāsa* easily tore their arguments to shreds. In support of their contention, the champions of renunciation pointed out that a mere statement of the fact that "I am *Brahman*" is not tantamount to the realization of *Brahman*. That *Brahman* can be realized only through long and arduous discipline of both body and mind, in peaceful solitude. That is, in the case of people immersed day in and day out in the belief that "I am the body" it is by no means easy to dispel the perverse notion, by occasionally repeating, "I am *Brahman*."

Therefore, the stage of *saṁnyāsa* wherein there is complete renunciation of desire and total avoidance of excitement, is indispensable to all true seekers of *Brahman*. To the enlightened who abide in *Brahman*, *saṁnyāsa* is a matter of course. The truth is, they have already become *Brahman*.

Abidance in *Brahman* is the unbroken flow of mental molds formed by *Brahman*. When the mind is engaged in a state of *samādhi*, how can the concept of body and other objects extraneous to the *Ātman* arise in it? Concepts of *Ātman* and of the non-*Ātman* cannot exist in the mind at the same moment. How can there be activities connected with the body in the absence of a strong attachment to such objects? As the enlightened ones abiding in spiritual knowledge (*jñāna*) are beyond the reach of activities, *saṁnyāsa* comes to them quite spontaneously. The advocates of *saṁnyāsa*, therefore, argue that during the stage of preparatory practice *saṁnyāsa*, in the form of the renunciation of action is indispensable, in the stage of attainment it becomes natural, that *karma* and *jñāna* cannot therefore exist in the same person at the same time. That the *karma* of Janaka and Vidura was merely the reflection of it and that only worldly people obsessed with the idea of sense enjoyment oppose the idea of *saṁnyāsa*.

It is hardly worth stating that Buddhism also insists upon monasticism and solitude as indispensable devices for preventing the perpetual flow of the senses and the mind toward sensuous pleasures and for weaning them to the quiet performance of spiritual duties. And that the wise prevalence of monasticism in Buddhist countries such as Tibet is the result of such insistence.

Practical-minded men have often asked in the past and still continue to ask, "Of what use to this world full of action, sustained by action, and propelled by action, are the *saṁnyāsin* who have renounced the world and its activities to live immersed in *samādhi* and *bhajan*?" To this question, the *saṁnyāsin's* answer is quite simple. Their very state of non-action is in itself a mighty blessing to the world. More than all the learned disquisition of erudite scholars, more than all their profound treatises, the liberation (*nirvikalpa samādhi*) of a *saṁnyāsin* touches the heart of humanity and elevates it to a higher plane. His desireless non-action does greater good to the world than the swiftest and the most frantic activities of the revolutionaries. What is more, *saṁnyāsa* is mightier than armies and is boundless as the sea.

## True Dispassion

Yet there is nothing wrong if a householder, residing in his own house, tries to realize *Brahman*, even as a *saṁnyāsin* does in his forest home. People of all castes and in all stages of life, in short, all human beings, are entitled to the enjoyment of spiritual bliss. It is their birthright. Spiritual realization is not impracticable even in the vortex of worldly activities, provided one has the necessary mental strength.

I am a *saṁnyāsin*, who has, after the acceptance of *saṁnyāsa*, made the Himalayas his abode; a great lover of solitude, engaged unintermittently in the contemplation of the *Paramātman*. I am a firm believer in *saṁnyāsa*, not only as a desirable stage in human life, but as the holiest part of it, one who looks upon *saṁnyāsa* as a miraculous means of converting worldly existence, which is generally regarded as sad and melancholy, into something full of bliss. I concede also that for certain people the very thought of the Soul is impossible until they have totally abandoned all distracting activities. That is all true, but in spite of all this I do not believe that householders are disqualified from leading a spiritual life or that people in various stages of life cannot meditate upon the Soul. In the midst of action, think of the Soul. Surrounded by wife, children, and grandchildren, still think of the *Paramātman* with devout love. Think, constantly, of the power that activates your hands and legs. Always use them to do things good and desirable. Do not allow yourself to be tempted by intoxicating wine. On the contrary, drink your fill of the Nectar of Life forever more and find everlasting Bliss!

The *śrutis* and the *smṛtis* amply prove that in the past it was householders, more than *saṁnyāsin*, who worked in the field of philosophical thought. Indifference to worldly pleasure is the chief requisite for spiritual advancement. Whether a man dwells at home or in the forest, if he has dispassion (*vairāgya*) he is a *saṁnyāsin*. One may put on the saffron gown and go on mumbling the *mantras*, but he is no *saṁnyāsin* unless he has the true *vairāgya*. There seems to be nothing absurd in the idea of a householder (whether man or woman) immersing himself or herself in Divine thought even as the great rishi*s* in their Himalayan ashrams did, provided he or she has the necessary discrimination (*viveka*) and dispassion.

# About the Authors

*Easwaran, Eknath*

Eknath Easwaran was a writer and a professor of English literature in India when he came to the U. S. as a Fulbright scholar. He
was the founder and director of the Blue Mountain Center of
Meditation in Berkeley. He taught meditation and allied skills to
those who wanted to lead active and spiritually fulfilling lives.
He wrote twenty-six books that are translated into eighteen lan-
guages.

*Jack Kornfield*

Jack Kornfield was trained as a Buddhist monk in Thailand,
Burma, and India and has taught meditation worldwide since
1974. He is one of the key teachers to introduce Theravada Buddhist practice to the West. For many years his work has focused
on integrating and bringing alive the great Eastern spiritual
teachings in an accessible way for Western students and Western
society. He holds a Ph.D. in clinical psychology and is a found-
ing teacher of the Insight Meditation Society.

*Schneerson, Menachem Mendelson*

Rabbi Menachem Mendel Schneerson, a revered leader and
teacher, was known throughout the world simply as "the
Rebbe." Although he was a Jewish leader, the Rebbe taught —
and embodied — a distinctly universal message. He called upon
all humankind to lead productive and virtuous lives, and calling
for unity between all people. His passing on June 12, 1994, was

met with great sadness — not only by the hundreds of thousands of members of the Lubavitch movement of Chassidus, which he had led since 1950, but by heads of state, religious leaders, editorial writers, and the additional millions who recognized his selfless leadership and deep spirituality, his dedication to education and to the betterment of society.

## Ramana Maharshi

Ramana Maharshi was one of the most significant spiritual teachers to emerge from India during the first half of the twentieth century, and remains widely admired. The article in this book is from the book *Be As You Are* which is a collection of conversations between him and the many seekers who came to his ashram for guidance.

David Godman, the editor of the book, has been studying and practicing the teachings of Shri Ramana in India since 1976. He is the past librarian of Shri Ramana's ashram and a former editor of *The Mountain Path*, a journal that propagates Shri Ramana's teachings.

## Swami Chinmayananda

Swami Chinmayananda, the founder of Chinmaya Mission, was a sage and visionary. He toured tirelessly all around the world giving discourses and writing commentaries on the scriptural knowledge of Vedanta, until he left his bodily form in 1993.

## Swami Ishwarananda

Swami Ishwaranada currently heads Chinmaya Mission Los Angeles. He was initiated into the order of *saṁnyāsa* on March 4, 2000 by Swami Tejomayanada at Sandeepany Sadhanalaya, Mumbai. Swamiji writes regular feature articles for the Chinmaya

Mission West newsletter. Before coming to the United States Swamiji served at the Chinmaya Mission Centers of Calcutta and Bangalore.

## Swami Jyotirmayananda

Swami Jyotirmayananda was born on February 3, 1931 in Bihar, India. He embraced the ancient order of *saṁnyāsa* on February 3, 1953 at the age of 22. He served his guru, Swami Sivananda tirelessly. In March 1969 he established an ashram in Miami Florida, the Yoga Research Foundation that has become the center for international activities. Branches of this organization now exist throughout the world.

## Swami Lokeswarananda

Swami Lokeswarananda was a senior monk of the Ramakrishna order and head of the Ramakrishna Mission's Institute of Culture at Calcutta. He spent more than forty years looking after destitute boys, running schools and educating the physically handicapped. He also initiated adult literacy movements in different parts of West Bengal. He attained *mahāsamādhi* on December 31, 1998.

## Swami Satprakashananda

Swami Satprakashananda (1888-1979) was a senior monk of the Ramakrishna Order of India. He was the founder-head of the Vedanta Society of St. Louis, where he lived as a spiritual teacher continuously since 1938. A graduate of the University of Calcutta with literary abilities, and clear understanding, he served nearly three years as associate editor of the monthly journal *Prabuddha Bharata* and later did the pioneering work in establishing the New Delhi Center before coming to the U.S.

## Swami Tapovanam

Swami Tapovanam lived for sixty eight years as a monumental expression of an ideal *saṁnyāsī* and a Vedantic teacher in the ancient rishi tradition, and was the guru of Swami Chinmayananda. Swamiji had a passion for nature, especially as it unrolled itself in the peaks and valleys of the Himalayas. He reported those travels in one of his books *Ishwara Darshan* which is an autobiographical sketch containing garlands of spiritual thoughts of a man of realization. Swami Tapovanam gained *Mahāsamādhi* on the 16th of January 1957.

## Swami Tejomayananda

Swami Tejomayananda, the spiritual head of Chinmaya Mission Centers worldwide is fulfilling the vision of Swami Chinmayananda. Swami Tejomayananda has served as dean, or *ācārya*, of the Sandeepany Institutes of Vedanta, both in India and California. He has written commentaries on scriptural texts, authored a number of books and translated Swami Chinmayananda's commentaries into Hindi. Swami Tejomayananda excels in expounding a wide spectrum of Hindu scriptures. His easy manner and devotional rendering of Vedantic texts has drawn many newcomers into the spiritual fold.

## Swami Tyagananda

Swami Tyagananda was a former editor of *Vedanta Kesari*, a monthly journal of the Ramakrishna Order. Currently he is the head of the Ramakrishna Mission in Boston, U.S.A.

## ABOUT THE AUTHORS

*Swami Vivekananda*

Swami Vivekananda was the foremost disciple of Ramakrishna Paramahansa. He was the founder of the Ramakrishna Mission. He became famous in the West through his address at the Parliament of Religions in Chicago in 1893 that helped focus the world's attention on the Vedantic teachings.

*Swami Yatiswarananda*

Swami Yatiswarananda (1889-1966), a former Vice-President of the Ramakrishna Math and Ramakrishna Mission, was a well-known spiritual figure in the Neo-Vedanta movement. He spent several years spreading Vedanta in Europe and U.S.A. His *Meditation and Spiritual Life* has been acclaimed as a spiritual classic.

## Pronunciation of Sanskrit Letters

| | | | | | | | |
|---|---|---|---|---|---|---|---|
| *a* | *(but)* | k | *(skate)* | t | *{think or* | ś | *(shove)* |
| ā | (father) | kh | (Kate) | th | third | ṣ | (bushel) |
| i | (it) | g | (gate) | d | {this or | s | (so) |
| ī | (beet) | gh | (gawk) | dh | there | h | (hum) |
| u | (suture) | ṅ | (sing) | n | (numb) | ṁ | (nasaliza- |
| ū | (pool) | c | (chunk) | p | (spin) | | tion of |
| ṛ | (rig) | ch | (match) | ph | (loophole) | | preceding |
| ṝ | (rrrig) | j | (John) | b | (bun) | | vowel) |
| ḷ | {no | jh | (jam) | bh | (rub) | ḥ | (aspira- |
| | English | ñ | (bunch) | m | (much) | | tion of |
| | equiva- | ṭ | (tell) | y | (young) | | preceding |
| | lent | ṭh | (time) | r | (drama) | | vowel) |
| e | (play) | ḍ | (duck) | l | (luck) | | |
| ai | (high) | ḍh | (dumb) | v | (wile/vile) | | |
| o | (toe) | ṇ | (under) | | | | |
| au | (cow) | | | | | | |

MANANAM BACK ISSUES
(continued from page ii)

*The Source of Inspiration*
*The Essential Teacher*
*The Razor's Edge*
*Harmony and Beauty*
*The Question of Freedom*
*The Pursuit of Happiness*
*On the Path*
*Beyond Sorrow*
*Self-Discovery*
*The Mystery of Creation*
*Vedanta in Action*
*Solitude*
*The Choice is Yours*

## Other Chinmaya Publication Series:

# T H E *Self-Discovery* S E R I E S

*Meditation and Life*
by Swami Chinmayananda

*Self-Unfoldment*
by Swami Chinmayananda

# T H E *Hindu Culture* S E R I E S

*Hindu Culture: An Introduction*
by Swami Tejomayananda

The Sanskrit word *Mananam* means reflection. The *Mananam Series* of books is dedicated to promoting the ageless wisdom of Vedanta, with an emphasis on the unity of all religions. Spiritual teachers from different traditions give us fresh, insightful answers to age-old questions so that we may apply them in a practical way to the dilemmas we all face in life. It is published by Chinmaya Mission West, which was founded by Swami Chinmayananda in 1975. Swami Chinmayananda pursued the spiritual path in the Himalayas, under the guidance of Swami Sivananda and Swami Tapovanam. He is credited with the awakening of India and the rest of the world to the ageless wisdom of Vedanta. He taught the logic of spirituality and emphasized that selfless work, study, and meditation are the cornerstones of spiritual practice. His legacy remains in the form of books, audio and video tapes, schools, social service projects, and Vedanta teachers who now serve their local communities all around the world.